More Praise for *How to Castrate a Bull*

"*How to Castrate a Bull* is two memoirs: one of Dave Hitz and another of the company he created. It tells of how Hitz founded and helped to grow one of the world's greatest technology companies, playing a key role in shaping the strategy and culture of NetApp through its early growth, the technology bubble, and into the new millennium. His story illustrates how a brilliant founder can stay with a company—playing a crucial role in keeping entrepreneurship alive even as the firm becomes huge and successful. This book tells the human side of that story, made all the more real by the memoir it records of this remarkable person. A must-read for those who delight in seeing genius in action."

> —Bill Barnett, Thomas M. Siebel Professor of Business Leadership, Strategy, and Organizations, Stanford University

"Lots of lessons for entrepreneurs, execs, and ordinary managers from the founder of one of Silicon Valley's most successful companies. Dave Hitz peppers his tale with light-hearted anecdotes and powerful insights. He's done an especially good job at describing how NetApp has created one of the country's most resilient workplace cultures. Highly recommended."

> —Robert Levering, coauthor of *Fortune*'s "100 Best Companies to Work For" list, and cofounder of Great Place to Work Institute

"NetApp may be the most successful high tech company you've never heard of. Dave Hitz is a founder and has written a book filled with insightful examples of the challenges facing any successful organization as it grows. The lessons he learned as NetApp grew from an idea on a cocktail napkin to a $4 billion company are useful to managers everywhere. Moreover, his candor and humor in telling these stories make the book a joy to read."

—Charles A. O'Reilly III, The Frank E. Buck Professor of Management and The Hank McKinnell-Pfizer director of the Center for Leadership Development and Research, Graduate School of Business, Stanford University

HOW TO CASTRATE A BULL

*Unexpected Lessons on
Risk, Growth, and Success in Business*

DAVE HITZ

with Pat Walsh

JOSSEY-BASS
A Wiley Imprint
www.josseybass.com

Published by Jossey-Bass
A Wiley Imprint
989 Market Street, San Francisco, CA 94103-1741—www.josseybass.com

Jossey-Bass books and products are available through most bookstores. To contact Jossey-Bass directly call our Customer Care Department within the U.S. at 800-956-7739, outside the U.S. at 317-572-3986, or fax 317-572-4002.

Jossey-Bass also publishes its books in a variety of electronic formats. Some content that appears in print may not be available in electronic books.

Library of Congress Cataloging-in-Publication Data

Hitz, Dave.
  How to castrate a bull : unexpected lessons on risk, growth, and success in business / Dave Hitz with Pat Walsh.
      p. cm.
  Includes bibliographical references and index.
  ISBN 978-0-470-34523-8 (cloth)
  1. Business planning. 2. Success in business. 3. Risk. I. Walsh, Pat, 1968- II. Title.
  HD30.28.H588 2009
  658.4'01—dc22

                                                                    2008043471

Printed in the United States of America
FIRST EDITION
HB Printing   10 9 8 7 6 5 4 3 2 1

Contents

CHAPTER ZERO

I am the product of a tryst in a squalid Times Square flophouse and was raised by a brothel owner and his opium-using wife. I am a high school dropout who started college at fourteen. My youth was spent hitchhiking and cutting the testicles off bulls. I sold my blood for money. I am an ordained minister and an atheist. I once ate dog meat and the still-beating heart of a snake. I made a billion dollars and I lost a billion dollars. I am presently employed as a shaman.

Or . . . I can say that I am the son of comfortable and educated middle-class parents. My father was an aerospace engineer while my mother took care of the three children. I went to college and studied to become an engineer like my father. I earned a computer science degree from Princeton in 1986 and headed off to Silicon Valley to write software. In 1992 I joined two colleagues to start a data storage firm called NetApp, where I still work today.

Both accounts are true. My story, like everyone's, depends on the circumstance in which it is told.

This book is a memoir of a company and of a man, because both stories are intertwined. NetApp started as an idea scribbled on a placemat, became a real business, and quickly grew to a Fortune 1000 company. Our sales are about four billion dollars a year. I began as a software engineer, became a manager, and eventually developed into a businessman. In a sense, NetApp and I grew up together. Being there from the very beginning has given me an amazing tour through business. I've seen—and participated in—venture capital financing, management shake-ups, hypergrowth, going public, economic disaster, strategic reversal, and recovery. It's rare for one person to survive such a volatile trip, seeing the whole thing as an insider, so I've tried to capture my experiences and distill lessons that may be useful to other businesspeople. I also want to tell a story that non–business readers can enjoy.

NetApp sells mostly to large corporations, so it isn't a household name—even though the company has thousands of employees, billions in revenue, and offices in over a hundred countries. Let me briefly describe what NetApp does. We sell giant boxes of disk drives to big companies that store large amounts of data—Internet e-mail, X-rays and CAT scans for hospitals, design data for new cars and computers—and we help customers manage all that data. If you've flown Southwest Airlines, seen *Lord of the Rings*, or driven a Mercedes, then you are an indirect NetApp customer. Major banks, telephone companies, and retailers around the world use our equipment to track customer records, which covers still more people. (I try to avoid getting too technical in this book, but there are more details in "Interlude: What NetApp Does" after Chapter One. There's also a glossary for when I do use jargon.)

I care more about themes and lessons than about chronology, but stories lose their meaning without a sense of time, so I divided the book into three parts: NetApp's childhood, adolescence, and adulthood. Childhood is about getting started, raising money, venture capitalists, and so on—plus one chapter on my own beginnings. Adolescence, in NetApp's case, was a time of rapid growth in the dot-com boom, and then a sudden, painful end to rapid growth. Adulthood is about becoming a grown-up company, selling largely to other grown-up companies. The bull of the title is a metaphor for risk. In some ways, the first part is about risk, the second about growth, and the third about success, but in fact, all three themes run through all three parts, especially risk.

This is my personal journey as well. In Part One, I am a programmer, spokesman, and company gadfly. In Part Two, I am a vice president with a $100 million budget and a staff of hundreds. In Part Three, I have no direct reports but influence NetApp's strategic direction by trying to predict the future.

There is more than one way to tell a story; however, this book is the best way I know to relate not just what I've learned but—more important—how I learned it. Let's start with my first business lesson ever:

Don't listen to my mother.

PART ONE

..

BEGINNINGS

1

BEFORE NETAPP

On Computers, Colleges, Castration, and Risk

My good fortune to be involved in technology came from not listening to my mother. When I was young, a family friend taught me the rudiments of programming, and I loved it. I read early computer hobby magazines like *BYTE* and *Dr. Dobb's Journal*. At fourteen, I bought a build-it-yourself mail-order computer called an IMSAI 8080. It had binary toggle switches on the front and little flashing lights. I programmed the lights to go back and forth. A television set was the display, and an audiocassette tape recorder was my first storage system ever. This was in 1977, right at the dawn of the personal computing era.

My mother seemed to feel that working with computers was not a serious profession. Perhaps she saw a matchbook cover that read, "You, too, can learn computer repair!" with a picture of some guy fussing with vacuum tubes and his butt crack hanging out. She made her opinion clear: computers were fine as a hobby, like ham radio, but you would never make that your career.

Computers challenged me, but high school did not. Some might feel that high school boredom is normal. My mother disagreed, and she worked to make education rewarding for her children. My younger sister had learning disabilities, but somehow, whenever we moved to a new location, or my sister graduated from one school to another, a perfect program for her needs was always just starting. Years later, I commented on this lucky streak to my father, who said, "Dave, you do know

Sordid Details Explained

The 42nd Street Fleabag

I was, in fact, conceived in a dodgy hotel outside Times Square. My parents had arrived in New York on their way to Europe. Bad planning and bad luck conspired to put them up in a low-cost hotel in Midtown. My father told me, "The place wasn't so bad," but my mother insisted, "Oh, yes it was," in that tone of voice that ends discussions. They went out for dinner, and by the time they got back, the drug store had closed.

That night in Times Square had to be my beginning. My father had been away on a business trip for a couple of weeks before, and their trip to Europe was romantically challenged due to a rough ocean crossing that left them both hopelessly seasick.

That was my first trip to Europe, and I don't remember a thing.

Opium

My mother was on a trip to India, and her tour group came to a little hut in the desert. Mom approached some wizened old men who were stirring a pot of liquid, and one of them cupped some of the fluid in his hand and offered it to her. She asked the guide if she should partake. He told her that it would be the polite thing to do, so she slurped the liquid from his hand. Only then did the guide tell her it was opium.

the reason for that coincidence is because that's what your mom did with her life?" Many school systems were not aware of the laws about what schools must do for students with learning disabilities. My mother made them aware.

My problem required a different approach: the law protects students with disabilities, but not students with boredom. My mom came across an article in *Smithsonian* magazine about young teens taking college courses at George Washington University (GW) in Washington, D.C., not far from our home in Virginia. We followed up, and at age fourteen, halfway through

Much later, at a family gathering, Mom was sitting with a particularly staid relative, and I took it upon myself to suggest that she tell us all about the time she did heroin. "It wasn't heroin. It was opium," she blurted out. She then reconsidered and said, "I mean, I don't know what you're talking about."

The Cathouse College Fund

While living in Virginia, my parents owned some investment property in Northern California. One day, the local sheriff called my father and asked if a man named Kentucky Wooten was his property manager. Dad had never heard of the man. It turned out that this con artist searched property records for out-of-state owners, rented out their property illegally, and pocketed the cash. He rented the ramshackle house on my parent's property to an enterprising woman and her two grown daughters, who established the property as the local whorehouse. Evicting anyone in California is tough, but tossing out pregnant women is especially hard. So, for the next couple years, at any one time, at least one of the women was pregnant, staving off any attempt to clear them out. My grandfather, who lived nearby, collected the rent for my parents until my grandmother found out and put a stop to it. Eventually, my parents did extricate themselves from being brothel owners, and later the property paid their kids' college tuition.

my sophomore year of high school, I started college: high school classes in the morning and college classes in the afternoon. I had always planned to be an engineer, like my father, but my adviser at GW felt that a narrow focus was bad for kids so young. For every course in calculus or physics, he made me take one in literature, philosophy, or creative writing. Even for an engineer, writing is a powerful tool; being forced to take classes with term papers was lucky for my later career. Never underestimate the power of a clearly written proposal.

This mix of college and high school worked well, but after a year and a half, my high school principal told me that I needed another year of high school math to graduate. Despite my three semesters of college calculus, he suggested pre-calculus, since that was the most advanced math class available. He also said that I'd never be successful without a high school diploma. That was an early lesson in idiot bureaucrats. I dropped out of high school to go to college full time.

GW taught me to love liberal arts, so even though I planned to be an electrical engineer, I didn't want to attend an engineering school like MIT or Caltech. I chose Swarthmore College in Pennsylvania because it is a liberal arts school with a solid engineering program. That didn't work out so well, because engineering prerequisites dominated my coursework. I could share a dorm with nonengineers, but I couldn't take many classes with them. Always read the fine print.

••

Even though I was at Swarthmore, I was still supposed to be a senior in high school, so colleges continued to send me applications. One was from Deep Springs College, a two-year liberal arts school located on a cattle ranch and alfalfa farm in California's high desert. The school had three hundred head of cattle and twenty-six students who worked the ranch when not studying. It looked crazy, but I mentioned it to my uncle, a Russian history professor at Cornell, and he said, "Deep Springs is a great school. If they invited you to apply, you must." Instead of trying to take liberal arts courses at the same time as engineering, I decided to go to Deep Springs for a concentrated dose. If you keep your eyes open, solutions often present themselves.

Deep Springs College was founded in 1917 by L.L. Nunn, a high-tech entrepreneur of his time. His story is a lesson in business. He was a pioneer in alternating current (AC) electricity, which powered his mine in Telluride, Colorado. In the late 1800s, there was a battle between George Westinghouse, who thought AC was best, and Thomas Edison, who preferred direct current (DC). Westinghouse was right—AC is what we use today—but Edison was a brilliant if unorthodox marketeer. AC was too dangerous, Edison argued, and to prove his point, he traveled from town to town, publicly electrocuting dogs and cats. Search the Web for "edison electrocute elephant" for an unsettling video. Edison even funded an electric chair company—AC powered of course—to promote the link between AC and death. L.L. Nunn convinced Westinghouse that a remote mountain mine was the perfect proving ground for this dangerous technology. It worked, and Nunn converted his mining company into a power company, electrifying mines across the rugged West.

Finding skilled workers so far from civilization was a challenge, so Nunn started a school to train electrical engineers.

That sparked a lifelong interest in education, and Nunn later bought a ranch in eastern California, two valleys over from Death Valley, and started Deep Springs College there. Deep Springs combines a liberal arts education with hard physical labor, desert isolation, and student self-governance. Students select the faculty as well as the next year's incoming class. The isolation and small size—just twenty-six students—create an intense community life. Nunn believed that ranch work helped balance intellectual pursuits. Adolescents reading Aristotle and Nietzsche can get a little full of themselves, but it is hard to take yourself too seriously when shoveling cow manure.

Ranch work can be risky. If someone gave you a dull pocket knife, pointed out a five hundred pound bull calf, and said, "Jump that fence and cut off his balls," would you do it? If you were fool enough to try, you'd probably end up with a broken arm (best case). Most people intuitively avoid foolish risk. But what if the ranch manager demonstrated the procedure and explained its importance? Castrated bull calves are easier to manage and fetch a higher price at market. Before Deep Springs, I could never have imagined performing rudimentary surgery on a touchy region of an enormous, angry beast; now I've done hundreds. Risk can be managed.

People are sometimes shocked that I've slaughtered cows and pigs for food. They say, "That's awful—I couldn't do it." But how is paying someone else to kill your food for you more moral than doing it yourself? The reality is, they could do it if they needed to. Ranch life demands self-sufficiency: it includes many jobs that you may not want to do, that you may not even be qualified to do, but when no one else is available, you do them anyway.

Years later, these lessons were surprisingly relevant in Silicon Valley start-up companies. Not the details, but the attitudes and styles of thinking.

••

After George Washington, Swarthmore, and Deep Springs, I was ready for a break from college. I spent the next two summers as a paid cowboy for Deep Springs. Between the two summers, I rented a room by the week in a seedy part of San Francisco and looked for work.

Short on cash, I spotted a place where you could sell your blood. What the hell, I thought, and got eight bucks twice a week for my plasma. Mom was appalled. My parents were not rich, but they were comfortable. Both came from families that had little money during the Depression, and like many from that era, they were savers. They would have taken care of me, but I wanted to make it on my own.

The state employment agency wasn't much help for landing a computer job. San Francisco wasn't as close to Silicon Valley as it appeared on the map, and the job agent knew nothing about computers except that they involved typing. She gave me a test, and I could bang out seventy words a minute, so she sent me to an insurance company where I spent the winter typing people's names and diseases on index cards. I'd rather have been shoveling shit. A winter of typing at Blue Shield gave me a very clear vision—better than most students have—of why I should return to college.

I applied to Princeton and was accepted as a physics major. Even though physics had been my favorite part of electrical engineering at Swarthmore, I struggled immediately. Princeton had multiple class tracks: physics for nonmajors, for majors, and for honors. I was in the middle track and getting middling grades. Meanwhile, I was taking computer classes just for fun. I talked my way into the "cutter course," designed to weed out students who didn't belong in computer science. The professor told me that I didn't have the right background and would not do well. Eventually he relented, and he later gave me one of only three A+ grades that he had ever handed out. When I got a programming assignment, I would rush home to start work. The problems were like fun puzzles. Physics homework was a painful grind.

Aristotle said that the secret to happiness is to find what you do well and do it. Getting a C– on a required physics course finally convinced me I was in the wrong place. I changed my major to computer science. Thank goodness for that bad grade. Had I been a tiny bit better at physics, I might be a second-rate physics teacher at a second-rate school today. My brain was not wired well for physics, but it worked great for computer science. This was before people saw computers as the path to riches. I didn't switch to computer science for the money; I switched because I loved the work.

The Secret to Success

Jeff Bezos, founder of Amazon.com, was my roommate for a year at Princeton. He also started as a physics major and switched to computer science. The president of Princeton told me that they were examining the room we shared for the secret to entrepreneurial success. In our senior year, we discovered a mummified mouse in an old couch that we scavenged off the street, and we hung it by a string over the entrance to the room. Perhaps that was it.

••

After Princeton, in 1986, I moved to Silicon Valley. Résumés are generally boring, so I decided to include "herded, branded, and castrated cattle" on mine, if only to see whether anyone actually read the whole thing. During one interview, I watched the hiring manager read my résumé. She scanned down the page and her eyes went wide. She cracked a little smile and said, "Management experience, I see."

My first real job was computer programming at a two-year-old start-up called MIPS Computer Systems, which designed computer processor chips. It had about a hundred employees and was growing fast. Too fast. This was my first experience with rapid growth, and it taught me how growth can cause pain and confusion. There were always new bosses, and communication was spotty and vague. Being a programmer at a chip company put me outside the company's core mission. I wanted to be part of a company where my work was the focus; I wanted to be on the cutting edge. After two years, I decided to leave.

In 1988, I joined Auspex Systems as employee number seventeen. It was my first small start-up, and product development had barely begun. Our goal was to build a network storage system that was bigger, faster, and more reliable than anything on the market—better, in particular, than anything from Sun Microsystems, which was the market leader.

Start-ups have a sort of pulse. You work work work: no customers and a limited supply of money. It's very creative and exciting because you are inventing from scratch. Eventually, hopefully, it all comes to a crescendo where you ship version 1.0. Then the creative work goes into a lull. You want to ship the exciting new features of 2.0, but first you have to do the bug fixes of 1.0.1 and the minor features of 1.1 and 1.2. But the features that matter most to customers often aren't the most exciting to design and develop. I had a knack for finding small projects that made the customer's life better. At a trade show after the 1.3 release, we had a poster listing four new features, and three of them were things that I had thought up and developed. If you focus on customers instead of technology, that lull becomes more interesting.

I went through several bosses at Auspex—I might have been a problem employee—but James Lau was the boss that stuck. Our skills and styles were a perfect match, his strengths aligning with my weaknesses and vice versa. For the past twenty years, James has always been my boss or my partner. I also met Mike Malcolm, who was brought in by Auspex's venture capitalists (VCs) to help resolve some technical disputes among the engineers. He was like a professor overseeing unruly graduate students, which wasn't a surprise since he actually had been a professor of computer science at the University of Waterloo in Canada. He had also started and been the CEO of Waterloo Microsystems, an operating system company that competed with and lost to Novell and Microsoft. Together Mike, James, and I started NetApp, but that came later.

In the early 1990s, Silicon Valley was an entrepreneurial wonderland, and for anyone involved in start-ups, it was tempting to start your own. Pen-based computers looked like a great opportunity. They were small, portable computers that you could carry with you all day and operate with a pen. Apple had the Newton, Microsoft had Pen Windows, and there were also start-ups like Go, EO, and Momenta. James and I observed that each new generation of computers created the opportunity for new start-ups. The people who quit their jobs and developed the first programs for PCs or for Apples hit it big. Our idea was to leave Auspex and develop applications for these emerging pen-based computers.

••

The decision to quit Auspex was hard. We were in on the ground floor, working with people that we liked and respected. Only a small fraction of start-ups even get funding, and of those, only a fraction survive to ship product, never mind getting profitable or going public. So it seemed like a big risk. Then I examined the situation from a different perspective. Several of my friends had left jobs to earn law degrees or MBAs, and nobody viewed that as risky. I figured that starting a company had to be at least as educational as an MBA. So my downside was the same as theirs—a year or two without pay—and my upside was much better, because we had some probability, no matter how small, of creating a successful company.

Castrating a bull is a metaphor for learning to take risk. Dropping out of high school, moving to San Francisco, switching majors, leaving MIPS—all were early experiments in risk taking. Each taught something valuable about what I wanted (for example, a career in computer science), or what I didn't (a career typing "osteoporosis" and "chlamydia" on index cards). You shouldn't take risks so dangerous that they might kill you. Or if you must, get lessons first. But even when not deadly, risk should feel uncomfortable, should push you beyond the familiar and safe. An ex-girlfriend arranged a special Vietnamese meal for me: snake prepared seven ways. As the guest of honor,

I knew I'd be the one to eat the raw heart. What I hadn't realized was that it would still be beating when I swallowed it.

The trick is figuring out which risks are worthwhile. Sometimes opportunities arise—but should you grab them? Was it really sensible to leave high school, quit a great job, or jump that fence into the bull's pen with a dull pocket knife? Those choices all worked out pretty well for me. You obviously can't accept every risk that comes your way—you shouldn't—but when I look back at the really significant turning points in my life, they all involved risk. That ex-girlfriend? She's my wife now. Perhaps *How to Choke Down a Live, Beating Snake Heart* should have been this book's title, but that seemed like too much. All in all, the snake was better than the dog meat.

James agreed with me that starting a software company to develop applications for pen-based computers was a worthwhile risk, and the two of us left Auspex in January 1991. One risk that never occurred to us was that Auspex might sue us. Nevertheless, our former boss threatened exactly that. He was upset with us for leaving and said that the other engineers had to understand that leaving was not okay. James objected that our new venture was not even remotely competitive, so Auspex had no grounds for a suit.

Our former boss explained, "You don't understand the legal system. Maybe I can't win, but I have more money, so I'll have better lawyers. If anybody else leaves, I'll sue you, even if they don't join your company. I have to stop the bleeding." That lawsuit never materialized, but the threat left a sour taste in our mouths.

In any case, we didn't have much luck starting our company. Venture capitalists were very happy to talk with start-up-experienced programmers like James and me; they were curious about what we thought and tried to hire us for their other projects, but they were not happy to give money to two technical guys without business experience or a CEO. Basically, they bought us lunch. Eventually we teamed up with another fledgling venture, but never got much traction. To make matters worse, Pen Windows, Apple Newton, and the other devices were not catching on. Today lots of people use smartphones and tablet PCs, but the hardware back then was too heavy, too bulky, and the handwriting recognition didn't really work. It was an idea ahead of its time.

It's hard to be at the right place at the right time, so perhaps the best alternative is to go to the right place and wait there. VCs never gave us money, but we met quite a few of them, which helped us understand how they think. I had saved some money from MIPS' going public, and we also took some consulting jobs to make ends meet, but my bank account was running low. It was almost a year since we'd left Auspex, and I was unsure what to do, when James called one day and said, "I just heard from Mike Malcolm. He wants to have lunch with us to talk about building toasters."

INTERLUDE
What NetApp Does

My mom periodically brings groups of her friends, mostly people outside the tech industry, to NetApp headquarters for a tour. Everything goes great until one of them asks, "What exactly does your company do?" Explaining high-tech companies is hard. I used to struggle, but now I have an answer.

NetApp sells giant boxes of disk drives—hundreds or thousands of disks—to big corporations with lots of data to store. Many movie studios keep animation and special effects on our systems. Yahoo stores e-mail for hundreds of millions of users. Others store less interesting stuff like financial data, information about customers and employees, or maybe engineering designs for cars and chips. Most Americans have indirectly used a NetApp product without ever knowing it.

We sell big boxes of disks, but the trick is, we don't make the disks or even the boxes they go in. We buy those from other companies. Our most important product is software that helps customers deal with the problems they have on account of all the disks we sold them. We protect data in case disks fail. If a whole data center burns down, we've got software that makes sure there's a second copy of the data someplace far away.

Recently we've been getting into more advanced forms of protection. If the Securities and Exchange Commission (SEC) visits your company and wants to see e-mails that your CEO sent five years ago, you had better be able to find them. We have software that makes sure your data has been saved and proves that it hasn't been tampered with. Or if you have private information that you don't want anyone else to see, even if they steal it, we have encryption to make it unreadable. Banks use our encryption to protect their customers' financial data, and the military uses it in Humvees in Iraq to make sure that secrets stay secret.

In other words, even though we sell big systems full of disk drives, mostly what customers like about us is that we help them manage all that data more efficiently and easily than our competitors. Customers can store lots of data in one place, be confident that it's safely protected, and manage the whole process with as little hassle as possible.

2

STARTING NETAPP

On Toasters, Angels, Resellers, and Ferraris

Mike Malcolm was a great mentor to me at Auspex, and I loved working with him, so I was excited to meet him for lunch at Hobee's Restaurant in Mountain View to hear what he had in mind. His idea was to build a storage *appliance*—a special purpose device designed and optimized for just one function: to let people store data over their network. It would be inexpensive enough for small workgroups to buy, as easy to install as a CD player, and manageable by users with minimal experience. Mike's simple concept would change the storage industry. This first meeting was in December 1991, and James and I quickly agreed to join up with him.

The simplicity of an appliance is very powerful. It does only one thing, so it isn't as flexible as a general purpose device, but for that one thing, it can't be beat. Consider cooking: with burners on top and an oven inside, a stove can make anything. In theory, a stove can make toast, but a toaster does it faster and more efficiently. For years the toaster was our mascot, because it has such a simple and elegant user interface: one button that says *Make Toast*, and one knob that says *How Dark*.

Our product would do roughly the same thing as network storage systems from Auspex. Both allowed users to store their files on the network instead of using the disk drive inside their computer, and to do this, both supported a network protocol called NFS (Network File System), which Sun had invented a few years earlier. This idea of a network storage appliance was the foundation of our company right from the beginning, but it wasn't till much later that we coined a term for the industry we helped to create: Network-Attached Storage or NAS.

We didn't feel that our old boss at Auspex had anything to be upset about because we planned to attack the very low end of the market. Auspex built large, expensive systems that could cost hundreds of thousands of dollars; we would make small systems that cost ten or twenty thousand. We expected to sell to small engineering workgroups at first, and over time we thought that network computing would spread to nontechnical markets like law firms and doctors' offices—our easy-to-use appliance would be perfect for them. (After the legal threats when we left, James and I didn't even consider going back to Auspex. I recommend that you not threaten to sue people who you might hope would return one day.)

We thought customers would love our appliance so much that we wouldn't need any salespeople. We even considered naming our company 1-800-STORAGE because anyone with storage needs could pick up the phone and order some. Recently, James and I stood on stage in front of our sales team—thousands of people—and explained that our original vision was to not hire them. Our plan was hopelessly naive, but at least we understood our lack of experience. In our January 1992 business plan (see Appendix A), one of our goals was "Obtain one or two senior marketing and sales team members."

Eventually we named our new company Network Appliance, which we later shortened to NetApp. We chose a generic name because we believed that the appliance concept could apply to many market areas besides storage, and we didn't want to constrain ourselves. We may have been planning a bit too far ahead: sixteen years later, NetApp still focuses on storage and data management.

••

From the beginning, I had a good feeling about NetApp. Two or three weeks after my first meeting with Mike, I went back East to spend Christmas with my parents. I kept having phone calls with Mike and James to discuss our plans, and after one call, my mom remembers me telling her, "This could be really big." By this point, she was much more supportive of my career in computers.

One reason for optimism was that we were modeling ourselves after Cisco. Before Cisco came along, people used regular computers—mostly workstations and servers from Sun—to forward data from one network to another. But when Cisco developed an optimized appliance called a router, they clobbered Sun in the networking business.

If you want to start a company, it's important to identify a problem that people are willing to spend money to solve.

People were spending a billion dollars a year on regular UNIX computers to do network storage, and the market was growing fast. Sun was the market share leader, and we hoped for the same success against them as Cisco's. We copied Cisco's business model and would later go after the same investors that funded them. Eventually, the chairman of Cisco's Board of Directors became the chairman of ours.

We planned to build our system out of the same cheap processor chips that powered desktop PCs. This was possible because we were targeting the very low end of the market and also because we weren't running a full-powered operating system like Windows or UNIX. This was one of the advantages of an appliance. Going after the low end was a good strategic decision for reasons we wouldn't fully understand for many years.

Finally, the idea felt good because it was right in the sweet spot of my experience. I had done related technical work in college, at MIPS, and at Auspex, so I had strong intuition about both the technology and the customers. Even as the juniormost engineer at Auspex, I had a track record of spotting features that customers wanted. By contrast, in our pen-based venture, both James and I always felt like beginners. We were trying to write an application to solve the problems of busy executives trying to manage complicated schedules, but neither of us had been a busy executive. A start-up that doesn't understand its customers is doomed. Even if the pen-based sector took off, we probably wouldn't have been very successful. In retrospect, it seems obvious: stick with what you know—design a product you would buy and use yourself.

Even before we raised any money, I started programming on my PC at home. We thought our design would be fast but had no way to prove it because our PCs were old and slow. I decided to sneak into Fry's, the legendary Silicon Valley computer store, to do some performance testing. I created a special floppy disk that would take over a PC, replace Windows with my special software, run some tests, and then display some data about the speed. I wandered the aisles looking for fast new systems, waited until no one was around, stuck in my floppy, and rebooted the machine. My program took only a few seconds to run. When it finished, I would grab my disk and find another machine to test. Whenever a salesman came over, I would say, "Just looking."

Eventually, a salesman caught me. He appeared behind me as I pocketed my floppy. "Can I help you?" he asked.

"This computer doesn't seem to be working. It has these weird numbers on the screen."

"Oh, really," he said, looking at the screen, perplexed. I snuck off to run more tests.

I still shop at Fry's.

••

This early work gave us something to talk about when we started looking for money. Most start-up funding comes from angels and venture capital (VC) firms. Angels are wealthy individuals, mostly guys who got rich from their own tech start-ups. VC firms are like mutual funds, but instead of investing in public companies, they invest in start-ups. Investors don't give you all the money you need right up front; instead, they invest in rounds. First is the seed round, which is just enough to get office space, hire minimal staff, and write a real business plan. Our January 1992 "business plan" was really a proposal for seed-round investment. A seed round can come from either angels or VCs. Next, if you are lucky, VCs come in with a much larger round of investment to fund development of the product, and then an even larger round to fund sales and marketing. Often there's one more round from either VCs or investment bankers to get to profitability, and then you go public. (This is the typical case; NetApp was different.)

The VCs that we met with struggled to understand us. "What does your box do that a computer from Sun cannot?" they would ask. "Nothing," we would say proudly. "Our product does less." Of course we'd talk about toasters and simplicity, really trying to help them understand our appliance idea, but they just couldn't get it.

Angels heard the same pitch that failed to impress the VCs, but instead of thinking our idea was risky and crazy, they thought it was exciting. In April 1992, we got our first four angels, $50,000 each, and used the money to incorporate, rent office space, hire an engineer straight out of school, and buy some Sun workstations to do our programming on. Ironically, we hoped to clobber Sun, but first we had to buy equipment from them.

We knew that we needed someone with experience in sales and marketing, and one of our angels recommended Charlie Perrell, who had been a vice president of sales at both Sun and MIPS. Instead of hiring our own salespeople, our plan was to work with independent resellers, companies that sell computer equipment from many different manufacturers. Working with resellers is also called *indirect sales*, and hiring your own sales force is called *direct sales*. (When you buy corn at the farmers' market from the family that grew it, that's direct sales; when you buy corn at the grocery store, that's indirect sales.) Charlie's experience launching and running Sun's indirect sales program in Japan felt like a perfect fit. He was a big boost to our business credibility, so we made him a retroactive founder, even though we had already raised some money and hired an additional programmer.

••

With angel money coming in, we needed a hiring plan. Fortunately, we had the benefit of hindsight. At Auspex, James was the twelfth employee and I was seventeenth; Mike had been involved with several start-ups. We sat down and went through Auspex's hiring order, writing down job titles and reporting lines up through about fifty employees. I also tried to remember the size of different groups when I'd been at MIPS with one hundred employees. Soon we had a respectable organization chart to take us through our first growth period.

Even though we had done the normal seed-round tasks— fleshed out our business plan, interviewed potential customers, hired key people into our team, even built early prototypes—the VCs still weren't impressed enough to reach into their pockets. Mike's past CEO experience had been in Canada, so he wasn't a known quantity in Silicon Valley, and they still couldn't get their heads around our "we do less" strategy. Later, a VC who rejected us told me it was one of the biggest mistakes in his career. After our success, he funded several other computing appliance companies.

One VC asked what had changed in the industry that made our idea possible. It was like he thought, *If this was such a good idea, someone else would have already done it.* At the time, it reminded me of the joke about the economist who sees a $20 bill on the ground but refuses to stoop down and pick it up. "If it were really there," he says, "someone else would have already grabbed it."

After the meeting, though, this question really made me think. What had changed? I saw several enabling factors: There was an emerging market, because network storage was becoming popular. It would be easier for a newcomer to gain legitimacy, because a new industry standard performance test allowed customers to compare systems from different vendors. And we could build a surprisingly inexpensive system, because desktop PC hardware was becoming fast enough to power a storage system like ours. I can't prove enabling change is always a factor, but finding it adds credibility to your story.

Meanwhile, our progress and our frugality impressed the angels, which was good because without the usual VC funding, we needed their money. Even more, we needed their friends. You see, when we couldn't get VC money, our original angels had a tough decision. They could either watch their investment swirl down the drain, or they could help us raise more money themselves. By the time we shipped product, we had raised almost $1.5 million from twenty-four angels. This was unheard-of at the time.

In a sense, you could say that the early angels got a bum deal. Instead of the one-time investment they expected, we kept asking them for more money and for introductions to more friends. I don't feel too sorry for them, however. When our stock price hit its peak, near the end of the dot-com boom, a $50,000 angel investment was worth $107 million.

On a trip to Japan to sign up sales partners, Charlie Perrell found some Japanese angels. One came to the United States to finalize the paperwork, and to Charlie's surprise, the man had $60,000 in cash in a brown paper bag. In Japan, it was common for people to carry large amounts of cash—in downtown San Francisco, not so much. The two men walked the bag from the hotel to the bank, Charlie nervous, the angel oblivious. At one point, waiting for a light to change, the Japanese man lifted his bag, and said to Charlie, "While I was gathering up *all this money*—" Charlie stomped the man's foot to make him shut up. They survived the walk, and Charlie said it was great fun watching the teller's eyes when they dumped $60,000 in cash on the counter.

••

Despite our success with angels, the lack of VC money kept us very lean. The only way to get serious funding was to design, build, and sell some of our products. With few employees and not much time, we dramatically reduced our set of features, abandoning many that we thought customers would like. That was a lucky decision. After we shipped, customers didn't complain much about the features we had dropped, and the things they did complain about weren't on our list at all. I now believe that when exploring new product ideas, it's best to ship early, listen carefully, and react quickly. It looks to me like Microsoft follows this strategy. They are famous for releasing first-generation products that everyone hates, but they quickly fix the most vexing problems and release again. By version 3, their products tend to be pretty good. It looks dysfunctional, but actually it's very clever.

We had a lucky disaster one morning when the entire engineering department—meaning all three of us—walked in to find that the Sun system where we stored our work had died. We expected to spend the day recovering from backup tapes, but then we remembered that for testing we had been copying all of our data to a prototype named Maytag. (We named all of our prototypes after household appliances.) Maytag became our primary storage system from then on, which gave us an excellent user's-eye view of our product and even more incentive to make sure that it worked well. In the computer industry, this is called self-hosting, or more colorfully, eating your own dog food. Moving onto Maytag probably allowed us to ship to customers three to six months earlier than we otherwise would have. Self-hosting was our eventual plan, but doing it early showed us that our system was more mature than we thought and helped us quickly identify the problems that really mattered. Eat your own dog food as soon as you can.

We shipped our first test system to Patrick Mulroney at Tandem Computers in January 1993, barely a year after Mike, James, and I first began talking about NetApp. Patrick was a system administrator in an engineering workgroup, and his boss was Mike's friend, which got us in the door. Going into his office and seeing his setup, I realized that he was our perfect customer. A Sun workstation sat on top of a cardboard box with three or four disk drives scattered about and strung together by cables. Our appliance could clean up his mess. He was a tinkerer and a good system administrator, and he very clearly saw the coolness of what we were doing. Earlier I said we did less than a regular computer, but we actually developed several very innovative features. Patrick's favorite feature was that our system rebooted in thirty seconds, instead of taking hours like our competitors' systems. He also loved the simplicity. I had written the user's manual, and it was only a couple dozen pages long. Sun's manuals filled ten inches of shelf space.

We built and shipped our first product with only eight full-time employees. It's true that we worked many long nights and didn't have much of a social life, but even so, it'd be impossible today to develop a network storage system in eighteen months with eight people and $1.5 million. Start-ups have raised over $100 million dollars to compete against NetApp and still failed. When a market is young, the rules are different—the bar to entry is much lower. If we had decided to attack Sun and Auspex's high-end storage systems with a me-too product, we would have been doomed, but instead we went after a part of the market that they didn't care about, at the very low end, with a completely new approach.

The Engineer and the Frog

On a walk in the woods, an engineer sees a frog sitting on a rock. The frog says, "Hey, I'm not really a frog. If you kiss me I'll turn into a beautiful princess." The engineer picks up the frog and looks at it.

The frog says, "Aren't you going to kiss me?" The engineer shakes his head and sticks the frog in his pocket. The frog pokes its head out and whispers, "Look, if you kiss me, I will do anything you want . . . *anything*." The engineer says, "Nah," and stuffs the frog deeper in his pocket.

The frog shouts, "I've got to get out of this frog body. I'll be your girlfriend for a year." The engineer says, "Who has time for a girlfriend? But a talking frog: that's really cool."

In July 1993, we shipped our first real systems—ones that customers paid for—and in September we finally raised our first round of venture capital. The VCs probably still didn't understand our technology, our market, or our business plan, but we made something that someone would pay for, and that they understood perfectly. Two prominent VC firms teamed up and gave us money to grow. Of course, VCs don't actually give you the money: you have to sell them a part of your company. When NetApp began, Mike, James, and I together owned 100 percent of the stock. After the angel investments, we were down to 75 percent ownership, still a majority. The first VC round took our share down to 43 percent. The Board of Directors consisted of the VCs and some of the angels, and since they now owned more than half the company, they had ultimate control. VC funding can be a bittersweet experience.

••

Our system turned out to be much more competitive for high-end environments than we expected. One way to test performance is to count how many requests a system can process in a second (technically known as *throughput*). This is what our competitors focused on, and by this measure, large Sun and Auspex systems were maybe five times better than ours. This wasn't a problem because, as I said, we were targeting the low end of the market. But another way to measure performance is to look at how fast a system can process one request (technically known as *response time*). If you think in terms of cars, it's like the difference between a school bus and a Ferrari. To deliver lots of children, a school bus is better. But to get one kid to school really fast, the Ferrari wins. Measured this way, our system was five to ten times better than the competition. They were the school bus; we were the Ferrari.

What nobody understood at the time is that Ferrari-style performance mattered for many high-end engineering customers. In retrospect, it seems obvious: power users want their results delivered quickly. Sometimes our system only took an hour or two to finish tasks that took ten hours on big expensive Suns and Auspexes. Programmers would run tests that sometimes took a day or two to finish. They would write software on Wednesday and not find out until Friday whether or not it worked. Our storage was so much faster that they would see results the next day or even later the same day. People doing hardware design and chip design had the same issue. NetApp provided an amazing productivity improvement.

It's true that we couldn't handle as many users at once, but customers could solve that by buying more of our systems. A key difference between school buses and Ferraris is that you can deliver more kids by buying more Ferraris, but school buses go slow no matter how many you buy. And unlike Ferraris, our systems were much less expensive than the alternative, so customers could afford to buy more of them.

One time, we got the chance to pit our box against the fastest offerings from Sun and Auspex. A software development firm called Synopsys hosted a performance bake-off and invited all three vendors to show their stuff. A team from Auspex came in with their refrigerator-sized machine and spent a week doing trial runs and tuning up their performance before running the test for real. Sun did the same thing. When it was our turn, I walked in with a box under my arm and plugged it in. The customer asked, "Aren't you going to tune it?" I replied, "It's pretuned. We're ready." We were so fast that Sun brought in a second team to tune for a second week, but they still couldn't beat us.

We won the contest, but we lost the order. For one thing, they were used to buying expensive, refrigerator-sized systems built with lots of custom hardware, and they couldn't believe that a small box running Intel chips could really be better. They wouldn't trust their high-end engineering data to the same technology that their kids used to play video games at home. At least, that's what we told ourselves—and it was partly true—but their biggest concern was that they didn't like the way we sold our products.

••

We had hoped that our indirect sales strategy, working with independent resellers, would be cheaper and faster than hiring our own salespeople to sell directly to customers. In fact, it was killing us. Customers were reluctant to buy from a small start-up that they had never heard of, and buying through a small reseller made them even more nervous. People will consider a start-up if they have a problem that they can't solve any other way, but they feel more comfortable having a closer relationship. We had modeled the strategy on PC vendors like Compaq and Dell, but their products were basically identical to PCs from IBM. The network storage appliance was newly invented, and people had never seen anything like it.

How do you know whether to change strategy or stick to your guns? We had stuck to our appliance vision when VCs scoffed, and we were right to do so. Was our sales strategy the same thing? Or were we refusing to change course

The Best Sales Advice Ever

Never buy anything from someone who is out of breath.

when the terrain demanded it? We did have some sales but not the groundswell we had hoped for. It was a difficult debate.

Mike Malcolm was leaning toward the direct sales model, but Charlie Perrell disagreed. That wasn't surprising, since we had hired him precisely because of his strong indirect experience. As much as I respected Charlie, I agreed with Mike that it was time to hire a direct sales force. Mike decided to try doing both at once. We would continue working with resellers, but also hire salespeople to call on larger accounts directly.

We needed to find someone with strong direct sales experience to head up the effort. One of our first salespeople was Kathy Mendoza, and she suggested we talk to her husband, Tom Mendoza, who had left Auspex as VP of sales a year earlier. Tom met with James and me, and he was very impressed with our product strategy. His meeting with Charlie did not go so smoothly. Tom thought the indirect scheme was doomed to fail.

Tom deconstructed our indirect sales model for Mike. We were mostly working with small resellers, and Tom felt that we were doing all the work, and they were making all the money. NetApp would help make the sale, and maybe help again later if there was a problem, but we sometimes got less than half of what the customer paid. Tom told one of our board members, "You're dead. This is toast. Great group of guys. I really think it could be a great company. But if you go down this path, you won't make it." Tom convinced Mike and the board that the math just didn't work.

We hired Tom for American sales and largely abandoned our indirect model, except in international markets, which Charlie would oversee. Tom joined in April 1994, and Charlie left two months later. After that, Tom handled sales.

Tom had been at Auspex when we won the bake-off at Synopsys, so he went back to them and said, "Now that I'm on the other side, tell me why you went with the Auspex system when it was so much slower?" The chief information officer (CIO) told Tom that his problem was NetApp's indirect sales strategy. If NetApp had been selling direct, he said he would have bought. Tom stood up, shook the CIO's hand, and said, "Congratulations, you're our first direct customer."

Tom had similar conversations at Cisco, Western Digital, and Cirrus Logic. Together those four accounts did $3.5 million over the next 120 days. Years later, Tom restarted the indirect strategy and it worked wonderfully, but at the time our appliance idea was too new and our company too small.

This would not be the last time that we completely reversed our strategy. You must be willing to admit when you've made a mistake. Spotting mistakes and then changing course can be more important than getting everything exactly right the first time. This is just as true in strategy as it is in product development.

••

Mike Malcolm was a genius. He spotted the market opportunity, invented the idea of a storage appliance, and it was Mike who called James and me, not the other way around. His years as a professor left him with a gift for guiding small groups of smart programmers. He drove us to design, build, and ship a product in less time than it took other companies to produce a brochure, and he raised the money to do it. When our sales strategy needed fixing, he hired Tom. Mike had been my adviser, my mentor, and my friend, so it was difficult and painful for me when I concluded that NetApp should fire him. Mike had no magic pixie dust.

INTERLUDE
Redundant Array of Pyramid Hieroglyphics (RAPH)

How do you store data so that it can be accessed a long, long time in the future? Like hundreds or thousands of years from now? On a trip to Egypt I learned how the ancient Egyptians accomplished this.

Some temples in ancient Egypt were for the dead, but others focused on the living. Those temples were partly religious, but they also functioned as centers of learning and healing, a sort of combination church, university, and hospital. The temple of Kom Ombo was for the living, and it used an interesting data protection technique. When running a temple, priests must perform different procedures every day of the year—different prayers, different offerings, different sacrifices. To ensure procedural compliance with data protection, the builders carved the operator's manual, a large table with 365 different sets of instructions, into stone walls.

Then as now, personal information required extra protection to prevent identity theft. Pharaohs made colossal statues of themselves, but if it was a good statue, a later pharaoh would recut the hieroglyph to replace the old name with his own. In response, Ramses II developed write-protected hieroglyphs. He cut them inches deep into hard granite. Expensive, true, but thirty-five hundred years later, Ramses II is one of the best-known pharaohs.

For most of the past two thousand years, hieroglyphs have been unreadable. But then the Rosetta Stone was discovered, with the same text written in Greek letters as well as hieroglyphics. To help people read your data in a thousand years, write it in multiple formats.

The data I accessed at Kom Ombo—with the help of a tour guide—was perhaps twenty-three hundred years old, but the pyramid of Pharaoh Teti contains hieroglyphic data over four thousand years old. Teti protected his data under tons and tons of stone (hardened storage?), but he also used redundancy. In his burial chamber, the same message was repeated down long columns. Many copies of the columns were repeated across the wall.

What data would you protect so that it could be read four thousand years in the future? The RAPH-protected message in Teti's tomb was this: over and over and over, it said, *Teti*.

3

CEO LESSONS

*On Pixie Dust, Decision Making,
Candor, and Going Public*

Mike was naturally upset when he found out that Charlie, James, and I had asked the Board of Directors to hire a new CEO. Mike confronted me about why we wanted him out. I told him it was time to have someone more experienced running the company. He replied that he had plenty of experience from being CEO at his previous company. That's when I said what I really thought: "Good CEOs have magic pixie dust that they can sprinkle on problems to make them go away. You don't have any pixie dust."

That just pissed Mike off. I was only a few years out of college and had never been a manager, much less a CEO, and I was trying to get him fired because he didn't have pixie dust. It was a tense time at the office, especially since it took the board almost a year to act. Fourteen years later, with much more management experience under my belt, I still think I was right.

The question of when Mike should step down went way back. We had looked for a CEO when we first started the company. Despite his earlier experience as a CEO, Mike was reluctant to "get back in the saddle," as he put it. He explained that the founding CEO of a start-up has the shortest employment life expectancy in Silicon Valley, and he said that the job came with two rules:

Rule Number One: Never keep more in your office than you can fit in a gym bag.
Rule Number Two: Always keep a gym bag in your office.

Initially he took the role on a short-term basis. He would be CEO for just a month or two until we got our first VC round. They'd help us find a CEO so that Mike could focus full-time on technology and strategy, more of a chief technology officer (CTO) role. Instead it took us a year and a half to raise VC money, and once Mike became CEO, he was reluctant to give it up. Whenever we raised the issue, he would argue that we shouldn't switch until . . . we shipped product, got more funding, became profitable, went public—always some goal at least six to twelve months in the future.

In our first eighteen months, we raised $1.5 million from twenty-four angel investors, often in $50,000 to $100,000 chunks. That was hard work, and Mike spent much of his time out of the office looking for money. Mike was most effective as a leader when he wasn't around too much and when the whole company could fit around a small table. We had disagreements, but we could work through them as a group. It was a relatively egalitarian environment. Mike was the first among equals, in the sense that he was the CEO and got to make the final decision, but most of us felt pretty comfortable pushing back on him if we disagreed, and Mike was generally willing to listen. I imagine his style was similar when he'd been a university professor guiding a small troop of graduate students.

The first VC round, in September 1993, brought in almost $5 million overnight, and that's when Mike's management style really started to break down. The influx of VC money changed two things: we started growing very quickly, and Mike no longer needed to spend time fundraising. I think it was the combination of more employees and more time in the office that pushed Mike out of his comfort zone as a manager. He was no longer the right leader. A couple of months after the first VC round—six months before we hired Tom Mendoza—James, Charlie, and I felt that change was necessary. We couldn't convince Mike ourselves, so in November we arranged a dinner with Bob Wall, who was an angel investor and also a board member, to share our frustration. We told him it was time for a more experienced leader.

••

We had eight employees when that first VC funding came in, late in 1993. By the following February we were up to employee 25, and by August, employee 50—six times as many people in less than a year. The more we grew, the more our decision-making process broke down. People would go into Mike's office to talk about a new idea or a change to our existing plans. If they were persuasive, they would come out and say, "The new plan is . . . " Those words began to strike fear in my heart. Mike was always changing the plan based on the most recent information from his most recent visitor. I was part of the problem too, because when I heard about a new plan that I didn't like, I'd be the one marching into Mike's office to argue my case, and I'd come out with a smile on my face saying, "The *new*, new plan is . . . "—striking fear into the hearts of others. The informal style that worked fine at five employees, and okay at eight, was dysfunctional at twenty-five.

CEOs have the right to manage by fiat, but they shouldn't do it too often. Mike struggled to keep the right balance as NetApp grew. He didn't know when to delegate and when to get personally involved. Bruce Clarke, employee number seven, was responsible for customer support. If anybody had a problem, Bruce took the call and helped them through it. He slept with a cell phone by his bed. When Bruce tried to start a customer newsletter, Mike wanted to review it, which was fine, but even after many drafts, it was never good enough. Bruce sent one version back with nothing but the exact changes Mike had requested, and it still came back all marked up. Bruce gave up. I had a similar experience with a white paper that I wrote to teach customers about Ferrari-versus-school-bus performance. The difference is, after accepting a couple rounds of Mike's input, which did improve the paper, I distributed it to customers against his wishes. As a founder, I was secure enough in my job to do that, but the new employees we hired were not.

Sometimes it felt like too much communication, other times, not enough. Tom Mendoza loves to give public praise when he feels it is deserved, and at one company all-hands meeting, Tom talked about Bruce's vital contributions to NetApp for taking such good care of our customers and presented him with a ceremonial clock. The award was Friday, and Mike fired Bruce over the weekend. Monday morning an e-mail went out explaining that Bruce was gone. We were all shocked and confused. (I'll spare you the details, but I don't think Bruce should have been fired. Later we hired him back.) One engineer didn't miss a beat. He sent out a company-wide e-mail with only one line: "Don't take the clock."

Seared into my mind, whenever I'm going to give someone an award, is this simple lesson: First check that their job is secure.

••

The only real power a Board of Directors has is to hire and fire the CEO. The board can give advice, but if the CEO ignores it, there's not much the board can do. The CEO is around all the time, but the board meets only once a month in start-ups or once a quarter in larger companies. If the CEO is going the wrong direction and won't listen to reason, then the board's only meaningful recourse is to fire him—or her, except at the moment I'm thinking of Mike.

Recently I was a guest lecturer at Stanford with Jeff Chambers, who is a VC. I took the opportunity to ask him, "When is the right time to fire a CEO?" He said, "You should fire the CEO the first time it occurs to you. If a founder or vice president comes to the board and says to fire the CEO, you have to take into account that they probably went through a lot before that point. They are there every day and not acting on a whim. Whatever is going on is a serious issue and will likely get worse." (Here, perhaps, the bull of the title is a metaphor for founding CEOs.)

That's not how our board responded. Instead, they told us they agreed, and they promised to take action, but month after month we would check in after board meetings and there would be no progress. Later, one of them told me that the strategy was to delay until the second round of VC financing. They knew we'd be adding more investors and wanted to include them in selecting a new CEO. Perhaps that made sense, but I wish they had told us. It took the board eleven months after that dinner with Bob Wall to replace Mike. We were on pins and needles the whole time, especially after board meetings, wondering whether Mike was still the CEO. I thought the board was full of wimps.

••

We raised our second VC round, $6.5 million dollars, in September 1994, one year after the first round. We were fortunate to get money from Don Valentine. No one in Silicon Valley had a bigger Rolodex file or better experience than Valentine. As the founder of Sequoia Capital, which had funded Apple, Oracle, and Cisco, and was later to fund Yahoo, Google, and YouTube, Valentine knew that good management made the difference between success and failure, and he made the hiring of an experienced CEO a condition of investment. I heard secondhand that Valentine was planning to replace Mike, and I requested a meeting to verify it myself. Valentine later told me that I was the only founder ever to do that. He assured me that he would replace Mike, but he warned, "Replacing a CEO is like a heart transplant. You find out pretty quickly whether it takes, or if there's an immune reaction."

At the first board meeting with the new investors, Mike distributed an agenda that included "Item #12: Cancellation of CEO Search." During a break, Valentine asked the other board members if they new about that. They didn't. When it was time to discuss item #12, Valentine spoke up. He looked at Mike and announced, "I don't know what you're going to do with the rest of your life, but this company will have a new CEO in two weeks, and you are not a candidate. What is the next item?" On that same agenda, item #1 had been "Elect Valentine to be Chairman of the Board." He obviously wasted no time taking control.

The Wayward Steer

At Deep Springs, the ranch manager told great stories. He described how they used to drive cattle a thousand miles from Texas to the stockyards in Chicago. In the herd, one steer would take the lead and the others would follow. This alpha steer became recognizable to the cowboys and was a great help if he kept his bearings. But sometimes this leader had a tendency to veer off to the side, taking the herd with him. Getting the herd back on track was hard work for the cowboys, so if the lead steer swerved too often, there was no choice but to shoot him in the head. Keeping him wasn't worth the trouble. So many ranching lessons apply in business.

Two weeks later, the board announced that Dan Warmenhoven would be the new CEO. Dan had been CEO of NET, a telecommunications equipment company. He had started his career as a programmer at IBM and worked his way up through the management ranks there and at Hewlett-Packard. He was an engineer at heart and completely understood what we were trying to do.

Dan was happy to take over, but he also recognized Mike's skills. Mike had built a product and a company with eight people and very little money. If he could somehow take a productive role, the company would be stronger, so Dan asked Mike to stay on as senior vice president of strategy. Valentine hated the idea. His advice to Dan: "Get the corpse out of the building before it starts to smell." Dan felt the potential reward outweighed the risk, but in the end, Valentine was right. Mike left about six months later and started yet another company, which also went public. Like I said, the man was a genius.

Thus ended one of the most stressful periods of my life. This chapter was hard to write, because it dredged up raw and painful memories. I was torn by conflicting emotions: loyalty to Mike, loyalty to NetApp, a desire to escape by quitting, but an even stronger desire to stay because NetApp was my baby. There were times I woke up in the middle of the night shaking. As bad as it was for me, I can only imagine how much worse it must have been for Mike. As you might guess, he and I don't talk much anymore, although I still have immense respect for him.

One time, though, Mike did ask for my help. We met for lunch, and he started describing a very complex legal situation. I listened to his story, and it slowly dawned on me that it would strengthen his position if he could show that he hadn't been the best CEO ever. I interrupted him and said, "Mike—correct me if I'm wrong, but are you asking me to testify under oath that I thought you were a shitty CEO?" He broke into a broad grin and said, "Dave, if there's one thing I knew I could count on, it's your integrity." I've been deposed many times, but that is the only one I actually enjoyed.

••

The difference in styles between Mike and Dan was immediately apparent. When Dan arrived, we had two competing projects for our next generation system. One was called "Bambi," based on an Intel Pentium processor; and the other was called "Godzilla," based on a DEC Alpha processor. The nicknames came from a campy short film called *Bambi vs. Godzilla*. (Spoiler alert: Godzilla wins.) The major issue was which project should ship first, or whether we even needed both projects. There had been many new, new plans.

Dan looked at the schedule and saw that—at that particular time—Godzilla was scheduled to ship slightly sooner than Bambi, although the risk of delay on Godzilla was higher. "The plan of record," he said, "is to ship Godzilla first and then ship Bambi. What I mean by *plan of record* is that's what I want people to work toward. We will review that decision after we've had more time to see how both projects are progressing. You can talk about other plans and other ideas all you want, but the plan of record won't change until the formal review."

It was a breath of fresh air. People could go back to work, safe in the knowledge that the plan would not change out from under them just because they were busy working instead of politicking. When the formal review came up, everyone with a stake in the outcome was in the room prepared. People presented what they thought would be the best plan: which product to ship first, or which one to kill. At the end of the meeting, Dan said he would like to hear each person's final thoughts. "This is a not a vote," he said. "I'm going to decide this one myself, but before I make my decision I want your advice." Dan announced his decision the next day. Not everyone agreed, but they felt good that it was a fair process and that they got the chance to make their case. Hearing different points of view is critical for good decision making, but if you want people to speak their minds, you must consider their advice seriously even when you don't follow it.

Suppose some explorers reach a large mountain and want to get to the other side. It's too steep to go over the top, so the only choices are go around to the left or go around to the right. Once the leader chooses a path, there's a great incentive to keep going. The alternative is to backtrack and go around the mountain the other way, but that may be equally hard. Sometimes you should reconsider a decision—if you hit a dead end or if you get new information—but you can't afford to do it every time you encounter a small problem. I felt like Mike sometimes ran his explorers back and forth so much that we couldn't make any forward progress. The plan of record was Dan's way of saying that we were going to stick to the same path for a while. It had a calming and stabilizing effect on us all.

I learned that Dan focused on the way decisions were made as much as he focused on the decisions themselves. Dan held an all-day staff meeting shortly after he arrived, and at the end he said, "I want everyone to rank our candor. You know each other better than I do. Did people say what they really believe? Did you? I won't ask you to explain your score, but I'm going to go around the room, and I want everyone to give a grade from one to five—five is good—on how candid you think we were with each other during this meeting." Dan felt that there was lots of bad politics at NetApp, and he wanted to quash it. He didn't mind if people disagreed with each other— that is a healthy part of finding the best path forward—but he wanted us to do it in the open, to each other's faces. We went around the room, and the average score was two, maybe two-

and-a-half. Dan didn't beat us up and didn't ask for details; he just said, "I see we have some work to do. This is important to me."

Some people think that *politics* is a dirty word, but not me. Politics is simply the art of making decisions in groups. It comes from the Greek word *polis*, meaning city. Any group working together—whether it has ten people or ten thousand—needs some mechanism to keep everyone aligned: that's politics. The question is: Is it good politics or is it bad politics? Bad politics is when people put their own self-interest ahead of the group's goals. To me, this is closely related to hypocrisy. You argue one thing (this is best for the company), but you believe something different (this is best for me). That wasn't our problem under Mike. Despite all the disagreement, I believe that all of us were honestly trying to do the best thing for NetApp. We just didn't know how.

I can't define pixie dust, but perhaps these stories have given you a sense of what it feels like. Two months after Dan joined, I sent Don Valentine an e-mail: "The transplant has taken."

••

When he joined NetApp, Dan knew that taking the company public was one of his goals—for one thing, that's how the VCs get payback on their investment—and he began preparation almost immediately. Mike had assembled a team that was fine for a tiny start-up, but it takes more experienced executives to run a public company. Two weeks after joining, Dan fired the first person from his staff. Valentine asked him, "Aren't you afraid of getting a reputation as a hatchet man if you move so fast?" Dan replied, "In this case, I'm more afraid of the reputation I'll get if I don't." The rest were less urgent, but within a year Dan had replaced everyone on his staff except Tom Mendoza, James Lau, and me. At that point, James and I focused on technology and strategy but didn't manage any other people.

Going public is a tricky transition: from private company, whose shares are owned by a handful of employees, angels, and VCs, to public company, whose shares are listed on a stock exchange so that anyone with a Schwab account can buy them. You start the process by hiring an investment bank. Helping private companies go public is one of their businesses. They find lots of institutional investors, like pension funds and mutual funds, to buy the shares, and they help you file amazing amounts of paperwork with the SEC and other government agencies.

I was excited to go along on the road show, which is a trip before the initial public offering—the IPO—to line up institutional investors. The meetings we had were surprisingly similar to sales calls I'd been on to sell storage systems, except the product we were selling was shares in our company. A salesman from the investment bank was in charge of each meeting. Dan and I were there to answer detailed questions about "the product," which was NetApp itself. Most of the questions went to Dan because he was the expert on NetApp's business details, but they had me along in case someone had a technical question about our storage systems. Mostly I watched Dan give the same presentation thirty times. In one week, we traveled to Los Angeles, New York, Philadelphia, Wilmington, Baltimore, Boston, and then New York again, telling our story five to seven times a day.

NetApp went public on November 21, 1995, and raised $25 million. It was just in the nick of time, because we were out of money. The IPO is really a large fundraising event. The company sells shares of itself to the public and uses the proceeds to fund growth. The IPO is also what allows the initial investors to turn their theoretical gains into hard cash.

The share price went from $13.50 to $20.50 on the day we went public. People often talk with excitement about how fast share prices rise after an IPO, but to me that's a sign that the investment banker screwed up. Think about it: the company is selling shares in itself, and it wants to raise as much money as possible. If the share price rockets up right after the sale, that means the company got ripped off because somebody else made all that money. It's like when scalpers sell tickets for way more than the face value. Sports arenas hate that, because they'd rather get the high price themselves.

Dan tried to convince the investment bankers to raise the price but had no luck. He asked Valentine for advice, complaining that he didn't seem to have any negotiating leverage. Valentine said, "That's very astute of you. You are right. All you have is your powers of persuasion, and the investment banking community has a peculiar anatomical deficiency: they have no ears." Ideally the stock would pop only 10–15 percent, but our 50 percent jump wasn't so bad: some dot-com companies saw their price jump by a factor of two or three within days of going public.

NetApp was one of the last "normal IPOs" before things went crazy in the Internet boom. We went public a few months after Netscape, but unlike dot-coms that had only "eyeballs" that they hoped to "monetize," we had real customers who gave us real money for real products. That's one reason we survived the crash of 2000, when so many other companies of our era did not. Our first CEO, Mike, had a saying: "Profitability is habit forming." Our second CEO, Dan, had another saying: "Profit is like oxygen. It shouldn't be the reason you exist, but you need it in order to accomplish anything else." In this case, both were right.

When we first started, our main challenge was to define NetApp. What should our products be? Who should our customers be? How should we reach them? In that domain, working with a small group of people, Mike was great. As we resolved those questions, the main challenges became growth, management, and execution. Both Tom and Dan brought us great skill in those areas, which was fortunate, because for the next few years at NetApp, the good news was that everything was broken.

INTERLUDE
Tom Mendoza's Lessons on Public Speaking

Over the years Tom Mendoza has taught me a lot about public speaking. I've watched him work, asked him questions, and reverse engineered what he seemed to be doing.

In public speaking, most people focus too much on the data that they want to present to their audience. Whenever I asked Tom for advice, he would always ask how I wanted the audience to *feel* after my talk. At first, my answer would be something like, "I want them to feel that they understand all the issues and details about our plan for—" At this point Tom would interrupt: "Feelings are one word. *Angry. Proud.* You know, emotions." You are allowed to have a small phrase describing what the feeling is about. Disappointed—in our performance. Proud—of our new release.

Next, Tom would ask what *action* I wanted people to take after my presentation. "If you don't want them to do anything different, why are you wasting your time talking with them?" he explained. If you've reached an important milestone in a project, you might want people to feel proud of what they've accomplished so far, but to keep working hard until they're done. If a project is way off track, the feeling of disappointment could motivate people to accept and engage a new approach. If a competitor is beating you, perhaps anger will help drive action. The trick is to choose actions and emotions that naturally reinforce each other.

When you are clear about the feelings and actions that you hope to inspire, then and only then—should you start to worry about the *content*, about what data to share to inspire those feelings. You could say, "I want you to feel excited about what you did," but it might work better to show the sales figures or product test results that prove people did a good job. Then the audience will naturally be excited. Or if the results are bad, naturally disappointed.

Presentations are much better when you start with feelings and actions. Good content is important, but it's only a tool. Feelings and actions are the goal.

At first, I struggled with Tom's method because I wanted to share too much information. Now I've learned to appreciate the elegance of finding the smallest amount of data required to drive the feelings and actions I want. For exhaustive detail, a Web site or white paper is a much better communication tool. Sometimes the action is go read the white paper. Even in a classroom setting, lectures don't replace textbooks.

Feeling. Action. Content.

PART TWO

..

TURBULENT ADOLESCENCE

4

HYPERGROWTH

On Goals, Doubling, Ancestors, and Pain

A company is most vulnerable when it has completed one major goal and not yet signed up for another: this was our position after going public. Dan said that an IPO is like graduating from college. For years you focus on getting that diploma, but then you leave school and it's time to go out and show the world what you can do. Dan was warning us not to be too pleased with ourselves. By some measures, NetApp was remarkably successful, but in the computer industry, we were something else: small and weak, with much larger competitors hell-bent on killing us, and customers who weren't big enough to sustain us. Going public is the beginning of a tough fight, not the end of one.

To survive, we needed new goals that were bold, profitable, and achievable. Dan held a three-day offsite for his staff, a meeting away from our offices where we could focus on planning the future without the interruptions of the present. The outcome was three goals that guided our growth for the next five years:

- Create a new market called Network-Attached Storage (NAS), and convince analysts to track it.
- Dominate that new market, with No. 1 market share.
- Double revenue every year for five years to a billion dollars.

The first goal was about being recognized. We believed that NAS was an important new market category, but it's one thing to claim that you've invented a new market and quite another to convince industry analysts that it is worth their time to study it and report on it the same way they do for computers, routers, and printers.

The second goal was about beating the competition. At that point, Auspex was our closest competitor, but we were growing so fast that we expected to pass them up before the analysts started paying attention.

The third goal was about our own execution, and it was bold to the point of controversy. When Tom Mendoza heard that his goal was to sell a billion dollars worth of equipment, his eyes rolled back in his head, and he practically fell out of his seat.

Tom believed in the company and the product, but a billion dollars seemed unrealistic to him. It was an absolutely enormous goal given that our revenue that year was only about $40 million. This company-wide goal would require fantastic products, successful marketing, and strong customer service, but Tom felt the burden most heavily because revenue goals traditionally belong to sales. I mistakenly assumed that Tom just didn't understand the math of doubling, but it didn't calm him at all when I scribbled down some figures and said, "Look, if we double every year for five years, that's well past a billion, more like $1.3 billion."

"Great," Tom said sarcastically, "the $300 million can be my safety margin."

Tom could have turned it back on me by saying, "Okay, Dave, we need the product to be thirty times faster." Then it would have been my eyeballs rolling back.

A few years before, we were concerned with hundreds of thousands of dollars and then with millions. Now Dan was saying we should talk about billions. "Can we do it?" he asked.

"Well, sure we can," said Tom, "we just need people we haven't hired yet to sell products we haven't built yet to customers we haven't met yet."

••

We had many reasons to believe that NetApp had a big opportunity. We had a track record of high revenue growth. Over three years, sales went from $2 million to $14 million to $43 million. Our initial market, storage for low-end UNIX computers, was growing quickly, and we found new markets as well. We added support for Windows computers, which roughly doubled our potential, and our Ferrari-fast speed let us sell to still more customers.

The biggest growth driver of all was the Internet. Many dot-com companies became great customers because they had so much data. They stored e-mail for millions of people, photos and movies to download, or pictures of products for people to buy. One analyst explained it like this: venture capitalists gave money to Web start-ups, and the start-ups gave it to NetApp. Early Internet customers included Amazon, Yahoo, AOL, Earth-Link, MindSpring, and even Hustler.com—the list goes on and on. In the Gold Rush, it wasn't the miners who made the most money; it was the people who sold them shovels and blue jeans. We weren't a Web company, but we supplied them.

As the dot-com boom progressed, this style of thinking drove NetApp's stock sky-high. Our price-to-earnings ratio hit 800 at one point, which was absolutely crazy. (I became, for a while, a billionaire.) Jeff Allen was our chief financial officer (CFO), and the stock market analysts wanted him to justify our stock price. "That's your job," he said. "I can tell you about our business and our growth, but as to what the market's doing, I really can't help you there."

The Internet helped us in a second, more subtle way: it legitimized networking for mission-critical applications—apps that absolutely must be available 100 percent of the time. In the early nineties, Ethernet, the technology that networks are built from, wasn't very reliable: good enough for e-mail or sharing files, but only a crazy company would trust it for applications that provide services to customers or collect money from them. Internet companies, however, had to depend on their networks. If the net was down, Amazon couldn't sell books. Yahoo couldn't provide e-mail.

This situation drove Cisco and other networking companies to make Ethernet faster and more reliable, and that helped NetApp. Remember, the "N" in NAS stands for network: Network-Attached Storage. Our products provided storage over the network, so improving the network improved our solution. At first, only Internet companies used NAS for mission-critical applications, but when the trend spread to traditional companies, it created a truly enormous opportunity for us.

Even with so much opportunity, it was fair to ask: How fast can a company grow? Despite Tom's skepticism, I felt that doubling to a billion was possible. The rules are probably different for different industries, so before the offsite meeting, I researched tech companies that sold computing equipment into data centers, as we did, and I derived some rules of revenue growth:

- You can reach $100 million within a year of shipping product.
- Beyond $100 million, doubling annually is the best you can do.
- Beyond $1 billion, 50 percent annual growth is the maximum.

You must also consider growth in terms of people. A rough rule of thumb for tech companies is $500,000 in revenue per employee, so a $100 million company needs two hundred people. At that size, the largest groups are engineering and sales, each with fifty to seventy people.

In *Guns, Germs, and Steel*, Jared Diamond describes different types of societies. The band is the smallest, with only a few dozen members, and Diamond argues that "the band is the political, economic, and social organization that we inherited from our millions of years of evolutionary history. Our developments beyond it all took place within the last few tens of thousands of years."

I believe it is no coincidence that the group size of our evolutionary history matches the maximum group size that can form easily and spontaneously in a company. A few dozen people can all fit in a lunchroom to talk and plan and form a team. Beyond that, growth becomes more painful. That's not to say it's impossible, but it is unnatural and takes hard work. If you double annually, then half of your employees have been on board less than a year. The big challenge is quickly absorbing them into your culture.

••

I was lucky to still have a job at NetApp. The title "jack-of-all-trades" is greatly valued in start-ups, but unfortunately, the entire phrase is "jack of all trades, master of none." Start-ups remind me of my time on a remote desert ranch: you need people who can do pretty much anything. As a company grows, job requirements get more specialized. Bigger companies have more masters and fewer jacks. Founders often leave after the IPO or after a new CEO, but James and I survived both.

Lots of people asked, "What's next for the two of you?" and VCs and headhunters called to lure us into another start-up. They assumed that we would be looking for something new. But when James and I thought back to our initial vision, we realized that we had much more to do at NetApp, and we wanted to see it through. We wanted to change the industry. We wanted NetApp to become a Fortune 500 company, like Sun and Cisco. We had built a foundation, but in terms of these big goals, we'd come less than halfway. Fortunately, we found places to contribute—James became CTO and I became "VP of doubling." Having two founders stay so long was unusual enough to make people curious. VCs sent the technical founders of younger companies to ask: Why hadn't Dan fired James and me? The secret was simple: We valued our customers and our company more than we valued the technology we had developed.

In the beginning, a start-up is all about new technology, but as it grows, other things become at least as important: customers, sales, marketing, and so on. In the end, a start-up is a business, and businesses must return profits to their owners. In a conflict between profit and cool new technology, profit likely wins. This isn't always palatable to a technically minded founder.

For me, developing our technology was a wonderful experience, but I also got a thrill watching customer adoption. It is one thing to develop technology that should work in theory. It is another thing to see hundreds and then thousands of customers actually use it. Some people love solving a problem, whether or not anyone else knows about it. Isaac Newton was that way. He invented calculus and then put it on a shelf for decades until friends begged him to publish it. His satisfaction came from the discovery itself. Newton was a genius, and there's nothing wrong with being wired like him, but if you are, then maybe you belong in academia or in a large corporate lab. In business, satisfying customers matters more than your favorite research project.

As VP of doubling, I would walk into a manager's office and say, "Right now you have ten employees. Next year it'll be twenty, in two years forty, and in three years eighty. Have you thought about how to hire seventy more people? Have you thought about how to organize a group of eighty people? Can any of your people manage a group of ten? In three years you'll need eight who can." My goal was to get people thinking big. If they couldn't, then we'd have to hire a boss over them who could.

The good news is that people don't worry as much about being demoted during hypergrowth. If your group of forty people is split four ways, then you become manager of ten. But two years of doubling will take you back to forty, and you can try again. If you weren't ready the first time around, it's a short wait until the next opportunity. Once people understand this, fast growth can help foster a healthy culture. Everyone has so much on their plate that they are willing to hand some off. (In game theory terms, hypergrowth creates a non-zero-sum situation in which everybody can win. I recommend the book *Nonzero* by Robert Wright.)

The act of doubling is not an annual milestone; it is an incremental process. Doubling happens every single day. The

The Grass Is Always Greener

In hypergrowth you must always be on the lookout for people to hire.

I once took a friend's daughter to a piercing studio to get her tongue pierced. The piercing technician had a shaved head and tattoos that ran down his arms and up his neck. His ears and eyebrows were riddled with holes, all filled with stainless steel hardware. He noticed my company T-shirt and said, "NetApp? You work at NetApp?" I nodded and he said, "Can I give you my résumé? NetApp is so cool!"

Surprised, I asked, "What have you heard about NetApp that you think we need a full-time body piercer?"

"I'm tired of this piercing thing. I mean, all of these idiot young girls come in and they want me to pierce their tongues, pierce their nipples, pierce their clits. I am so tired of teen nipples and tongues and—what I love is IT."

"IT? You mean information technology?"

"Yeah. I'm the guy that put up the Web site for this shop and I can do Linux and Apache. My favorite operating system is Linux 2.4. I would love to work for NetApp."

Perhaps he interpreted my shocked expression as skepticism that his Linux experience was sufficiently broad, because he immediately said, "Oh oh oh, not a problem. I can do Windows too."

I gave him my card.

key is to stay focused. A trick that helps people think about annual doubling is to break it into quarterly goals. To double in a year, you must grow by 20 percent each quarter—actually it's 18.9 percent, but close enough. Instead of focusing on the distant, giant numbers, I would focus on the next two quarters. "You've got twenty people today. That's twenty-four in three months and twenty-nine in six. Do you have nine people in your hiring pipeline?" I practiced doing the math for 20 percent growth in my head. Managers who weren't on track for the next two quarters would never succeed at doubling in a year.

••

The first lesson of hypergrowth is *Everything is always broken.* Relax, because it's a good thing. Of course, there are good problems and bad problems. We need more office space. Our demand exceeds our production capacity. We have too many orders to process. I love to hear problems like this. On the other hand: Everyone is quitting. Sales are down. Our investors are dissatisfied. Not good.

Problems during doubling tend to be the good kind, and pointing that out to people can help morale. Our VP of engineering at the time, Helen Bradley, did this. When people complained about sharing small cubes that were designed for just one person, Helen said, "Be careful what you wish for. My last company had plenty of space—because people were being laid off."

Systems and processes that work well for a small company often fail for a larger one. Accounting software designed for $10 million in revenue didn't scale to $100 million. We bought the small-company version anyway, knowing it would break soon, because the one for big companies was too expensive. Even with a giant discount, we couldn't have afforded the customization required to install it or the people to operate it. Companies in hypergrowth are rare, so application vendors don't optimize for their needs. The result is lots of problems.

It is tempting to fix every problem, but that is a mistake. The old saying "a stitch in time saves nine" is fine if you only have one problem. But what if you have a thousand problems? It would take a thousand stitches to prevent them all. Better to fix the few that are deadly and ignore the rest. Don't fix a problem because it's painful; fix it because it impedes growth.

We accumulated lots of painful problems, and people naturally complained. "What moron designed this inadequate system?" It does not inspire confidence if new people believe they were brought into a company to clean up someone else's mess. I tried to help them understand that even good systems break under the strain of doubling. Whoever put the system in place probably did the best they could with the resources they had.

Brian Ehrmantraut was our seventeenth employee, and he focused on making NetApp more mature. He wrote a process manual documenting the steps required to accomplish various tasks. Years later, Brian was working on a problem and came up with an innovative solution. A much more recent employee told him, "We can't do that. It's not how NetApp does business."

"What are you talking about?" Brian asked. The employee went to the shelf, grabbed a book, and flipped it open: "See, it says right here that we have to do it this way."

Brian looked at him and said, "Don't give me this bullshit. We were a thirty-person company when that was written.

Now we have three hundred. Besides, I wrote that procedure myself."

When new people were fixing the problems of the past, I cautioned them not to complain too loudly about the "moron who designed this system." I said, "You'll design a replacement system, and after two more years of growth, the moron will turn out to be you." Respect your ancestors, and perhaps your descendants will respect you.

With so many new employees coming in, we invested heavily in training. Once a month we invited all new employees to spend a day with the executive staff. Most of the executives described the goals for their particular part of the company, but I wanted to give people a sense of how hypergrowth feels. I tried to inoculate them against the pain by warning them about it. Growth is exciting, and it creates opportunity—not only for the company but also for people's careers. They can withstand the pain more easily if they see it as a natural side effect of something healthy.

One thing I fought during those talks was simple disbelief. When NetApp was 250 people, I put up a spreadsheet showing that in three years we would have 2,000 people. It was natural for people to doubt, but if they don't believe, they won't even try, so I told stories about other companies that had done it, like Oracle, Cisco, and Sun. Many ingredients are required to sustain such fast growth—good products, good sales, a large enough market opportunity—but one critical factor is *deciding* to grow.

••

Given the pain of doubling, many wondered why NetApp should grow so fast. Couldn't we serve our customers better if we grew at a more reasonable rate? I replied that growth for growth's sake is not a worthy goal, but we could never lead the industry we helped create by remaining small. We might not even survive.

In *Inside the Tornado*, Geoffrey Moore describes the difference between Oracle, which you've probably heard of, and their early competitor Ingres, which you probably haven't. "What set Oracle apart from Ingres," says Moore, "was that Larry Ellison [the CEO] drove for 100 percent growth while Ingres 'accepted' 50 percent growth. To garner that 100 percent growth he simply doubled the size of his sales force every year." Ingres had a different theory: "We simply cannot grow any faster than 50 percent and still adequately serve our customers." With such different growth rates, Oracle killed Ingres in no time. Oracle got so much bigger, so much faster, that they out-invested Ingres on every front. Trying to double may seem risky, but not trying can be even more dangerous. You can't serve customers at all if you are dead.

Having decided to double, we optimized the whole company for growth, and we succeeded. By 2001, we had 2,400 employees and $1 billion in revenue. Our motto during this era was *Double or Die*.

There is a deep link between hypergrowth and culture. In hypergrowth, new employees (and new problems) arrive so fast that detailed planning can't possibly succeed. You set high-level goals and trust people to do the right thing. All my personal experience was in start-ups, and the dot-com customers I spent time with were also growing very fast, so I assumed that this model was best for everyone. I couldn't understand why big old companies couldn't see the light and adopt our (obviously superior) culture.

My first experience with "stodgy old companies" occurred when we started selling to them in the late 1990s. I went to visit companies like Ford and General Electric, and their culture baffled me. We would talk to information technology (IT) people managing millions of dollars of budget, but they had no autonomy whatsoever. As near as I could tell, their companies had teams of accountants with green eyeshades and sharpened pencils who dominated every decision. Crazy!

The more I learned about these companies, the more I understood the logic of their structure, and that helped me understand our own culture. In a hypergrowth company, you optimize everything for growth. Trimming IT spending from 5 percent of revenue to 4 percent might seem like a good plan, but if it slows your growth, you've made a terrible mistake. Better to waste a little money and keep on doubling. To achieve this, you design a decentralized culture. You help people understand the big picture, warn them of the challenges, and then turn them loose. Sometimes they screw up, but more often they find and fix problems that never would have occurred to you. Things are changing so fast that centralized planning is impossible. Instead of focusing on process and control, you focus on trust and enablement.

It is completely different for a mature company that dominates its market and doesn't expect much growth. If you can't increase revenue, then to improve profitability you must reduce costs. In this case, trimming IT spending will increase earnings by the same amount, which should drive up your share price. The same strategy that was a terrible mistake in hypergrowth makes great sense here. When things aren't changing very fast, centralized control can work. If you identify a cost savings, standardize it and push it through the whole organization. In other words, put the people with pencils and eyeshades in charge.

••

When the stock market crashed in 2000, NetApp's stock fell from $150 a share to $6 in less than a year. *Fortune* published an article called "The Forty Biggest Losers," which listed the individuals who lost the most money in the crash. I lost over a billion dollars and was number thirty-two on the list. When my assistant Kathy Bittner saw that, she marched into my office, held up the article, and said, "This makes me ashamed to work for you. Here are all the biggest losers, and you can't even make the top twenty." One of Kathy's jobs is to keep my ego in check. Another friend helped out too. He came up to me and said, "Hey Dave, did I ever tell you that I used to know a billionaire?"

The dot-com boom of the 1990s was a classic market bubble. Everyone sensed that the Internet was going to change everything, and in some ways it has, but there was no justification for the crazy stock prices. The crash hit Internet companies first, but then spread quickly to anyone that sold to them. Seventy percent of our revenue came from Internet and technology companies, so their pain became ours.

Now the analysts wanted our CFO, Jeff Allen, to tell them how quickly the stock market would bounce back. Would it be a V-shaped graph or a U-shaped graph? Jeff said, "I know what you want to hear, but I'm not going to blow sunshine up your ass. I think the market looks flattish. L-shaped." Nobody wanted that news, but I was proud of Jeff. He wouldn't make stuff up back when the stock was so high, and he still wouldn't now that it was so low.

We had designed NetApp for growth, and when the growth stopped, everything broke, but this time in a bad way. Our highest quarter was $290 million in sales, and based on the 20 percent per quarter rule, we expected to be well over $400 million per quarter six months later. We were hiring people based on that assumption. Instead, our sales six months later were under $200 million—less than half what we'd been counting on.

Dan didn't want to do layoffs. He had done layoffs at his previous company, and I think he still felt guilty. But at the same time, he had very strong feelings about staying profitable. He felt that posting losses would be so damaging to NetApp, at a time when many companies were failing, that it would put everyone's job at risk. Dan let profits go all the way down to zero, but when they threatened to go negative, he wouldn't postpone any longer. Some companies announced a layoff and then took months to plan and execute. That approach hurt morale, and people spent so much time worrying about losing their jobs that nobody got anything done. We decided to act quickly.

We announced layoffs one day and did them the next. The day of the announcement we had a training session for all the managers who would be laying people off. They had many questions, like "Do I ask them to clear out their desks right away or let them come back later or what?" My answer was "Why not ask the person what they prefer?" We had a lawyer to answer legal questions, but I told the group, "The laws on this probably fill twenty books, and you'll never learn it all by tomorrow. My advice is to treat everybody like a human being, the way you would want to be treated in this situation, and the odds are that it is probably legal. I trust you."

••

The dot-com era was like a giant wave. It lifted us, and carried us, and when it set us down, NetApp was a completely different company—a large company, a billion in revenue, and we were helping even larger companies solve some of their most important problems, a far cry from the small workgroups that we started with.

The wave analogy encourages humility. Imagine you are surfing, and you spot the biggest wave ever. You decide to catch it, and you have the best ride of your life. You can be proud of spotting the wave, and of deciding to catch it, but don't be proud of the wave itself. We didn't invent the Web or even predict the Web, but we saw it coming and decided to catch it. I'm proud of how well we rode.

The key lesson is that change creates opportunity. With change, customers encounter new problems, and although they hate working with start-ups, they will if their problems force them to. As a small company, I'd much rather target a turbulent $1 billion market than a stable $10 billion one. If the chaotic market is adjacent to a giant stable one, so much the better; with luck, the chaos may spread. The Internet was a rare opportunity, but such opportunities favor the prepared, so I hope that describing our experience will help you spot the wave of a lifetime in your own industry.

Perhaps it is the nature of hypergrowth to always end in a thud. To optimize for growth, you assume it won't stop. You

The Stupidest Business Plan

The basic argument of the Stupidest Business Plan goes like this: "Coca-Cola sells $30 billion a year. If I could convince 1 percent of those people to buy my product, Koka-Kola, that would be $300 million. That's a major company!"

It sounds good at first but ignores the question of how to get 1 percent of Coke's shelf space or customers. Why would happy Coke customers switch? Targeting an entire giant market makes no sense. You should either target an unhappy subset, or a group that isn't buying at all. That's the dollar figure to talk about.

Ben & Jerry's did this in the ice cream market. They didn't try to grab 1 percent with an identical product. Within the niche of especially rich and tasty ice creams, they found a subniche that was willing to pay more for ice cream made by a company with high social values. Identifying a tiny new niche is better than trying to take on a giant market with a me-too product.

The rules are different for the market share leader. In a meeting with Coca-Cola, I asked how they can possibly expand, given that every store, cafeteria, and break room already has a Coke machine. The response: "Our CEO says our mission is not complete until every sink on the planet has Hot, Cold, and Coke."

hire well in advance, because new people can take six months or more to get fully up to speed. To double revenue, you double the sales force. We operated like this for seven years in a row. The problem is, when the end arrives, you will almost certainly overshoot. Slowing too soon is dangerous, so you just keep going. Thud.

We survived the crash because a few years earlier we had begun selling to several new market areas, like banks, telephone companies, and the federal government. To recover, we shifted our focus much more strongly toward these new segments. I am very interested in how strategy changes at the transition from one period in a company's history to its next. The details are a topic for Part Three of this book, but I am calling attention to it here because this transition is so important to NetApp's maturation.

NetApp's turbulent adolescence began with hypergrowth and ended with the crash. The next chapter focuses on this same period, but from the perspective of how values and culture created a company resilient enough to survive.

INTERLUDE
How to Fail in Executive Staff Presentations

Imagine this scenario: An old friend rushes up and says, "You wouldn't believe the amazing car I saw yesterday. Twenty-five years old, but the paint is perfect, and it runs like a charm." You ask him what his point is, but he keeps talking about the car. "It's not expensive now, but a classic like this is sure to go up in value." On and on he goes.

You look at your watch, and your friend suddenly says, "Wait! This car is for sale on eBay. I want you to buy it and lease it to me. It's a great investment for you." There you are, two minutes from your next meeting. How do you react? You need time to think, but he says, "The auction ends today. I gave you all the data you need. My facts prove that this is a great deal. You need to decide right now."

Presenters in executive staff meetings often trigger this feeling, and I hate it. The meeting agenda has forty-five minutes on a vague but interesting topic (for example, Classic Cars). For forty-two minutes the presenter shares various facts and figures, and then—with three minutes left—the presenter puts up a complex proposal (say, Automotive Investment and Leasing) and asks for approval. You should know that presentations like this almost never go well.

This sounds idiotic, maybe even sneaky and underhanded, but I think people have good intentions. They believe they have an airtight case, and they want to present all the evidence so that when they get to the conclusion, everyone will immediately see that their plan is perfect. Kind of like in detective shows where the hero reveals the evidence point by point and then dramatically identifies the killer. The genius detective technique is great in movies, but in presentations it leaves the audience wanting to go back and reexamine the evidence.

The problem is lack of context. The presentation may be interesting and informative, but if you don't know what the conclusion is, it is almost impossible to judge how well the evidence supports it. To return to my simple analogy, if you had known it was about *buying* the car, you might have asked all sorts of questions. What is the Blue Book value? Has it been inspected? How many miles? You can't evaluate the arguments and ask the right questions unless you know where the presenter is taking you.

Perhaps people want to postpone the pain of rejection till the end of the meeting. But it's better to find out concerns or objections right away, because that's when the conversation gets interesting. Maybe you'll change people's minds. Maybe you'll find alternatives that do work. Get shot down early and use the time to recover or to prepare for the next attempt.

Here is my advice: Always start with the conclusion. Somewhere in your presentation you have a conclusion slide that summarizes the proposal you hope to get approved. Put that slide first. Maybe you can get away with one slide of background information before the conclusion, but any more than that and you are probably trying to be a genius detective. As I said, those presentations almost never go well.

5

VALUES AND CULTURE

On Dilbert, Drooling, Lies, and Game Theory

Dan's first attempt to create a list of company values, shortly after he joined NetApp, failed miserably. We proposed the idea at an all-hands meeting, and a woman named Florence Chan stood up and asked, "How will these values be used against us?" She'd had a particularly bad experience with company values at a prior employer, but I have to admit that the meeting made me uncomfortable as well. Words like *culture* and *values* had Dilbert-ish connotations. I hate it when people tell me what my beliefs should be, so it seemed wrong—even hypocritical— for me to tell other people what theirs should be. People either believe something or they do not. Can their employer change that? What does it even mean for a company to have values? The whole thing felt strange and unpleasant to me, and I wasn't the only one.

The discussion went on the back burner, but Dan wasn't going to let it drop. When he had joined NET, his employer before NetApp, one of their large customers wasn't paying their bills. Or rather, they'd pay some bills but not others. Dan met with them to find out why. They reviewed purchase orders together and found one that hadn't been paid. The customer looked carefully at the PO and said, "That's not my signature. I never ordered that system."

NET was riddled with fraud: the sales team was creating fake orders and sending systems to secret warehouses instead of to real customers. When the scheme unraveled, the CEO was fired, the CFO was fired, and the head of sales was fired. Dan had joined as chief operating officer (COO), but the board asked him to be CEO and clean up the mess. He had to cope with an SEC investigation, a shareholder class action lawsuit, and the stock plummeting from $35 to $6. Worst of all, the fraud made it look as though the company's growth was much greater than it really was, and as a result, they had hired more people than they could afford. They had to lay off a third of the workforce. The experience left Dan with strong feelings about values, or the lack thereof.

A year after that first failed attempt at NetApp values, Dan broached the subject again at an offsite meeting with his staff. I was uncomfortable at first, but to his credit, he didn't try to tell me what to believe. Instead, he talked about what was important to him and his aspirations for the kind of company that he hoped NetApp would become. He shared the fraud story— the kind of company he hoped we would not become. And he encouraged his staff to share their thoughts as well. In other words, he sort of eased us into assembling a list of values.

Some of our values might appear on any company's list: trust, integrity, teamwork, and so on. At first, it seemed odd to have the same items, but then I thought, what if someone were writing the constitution for a new country? It wouldn't bother me at all if they included Freedom of the Press or Freedom of Religion. In fact, I'd recommend it. As we talked, it became clear that we also had values that were different from those of other companies. Given our appliance philosophy, James and I were adamant about simplicity, not just for the product but for how we ran NetApp, so we added that. At the very end of the discussion, Tom looked at our tentative list and said, "Maybe this touchy-feely stuff is important—it's not that I disagree with anything here—but where does it say that we're actually going to *do* something? What's the point of having good values if we fail as a company?" So we finished off our list with "Get Things Done!" (See Appendix B for the complete set.)

At first I was still uncomfortable talking to people about NetApp values, but over the years my perspective has changed. It's appropriate for Dan's staff to define the kind of company we want to build and to say what behaviors are acceptable or not. The values are an attempt to capture that. The staff has diverse views on religion and politics—we don't want to influence those kinds of beliefs—but employees who don't agree with the kind of work environment we are trying to create may find that they don't fit into NetApp's culture. If the disagreement is too strong, they might be better off leaving. This may seem like a subtle distinction, but even though I'm uncomfortable telling people what their beliefs should be, I'm completely comfortable letting them know what ours are, so they can decide whether or not they want to join in.

Just writing down good values isn't worth much. It wouldn't surprise me if Enron had a long and lofty list. Company values only work if the leaders say, "These are things that I really do believe. If I violate them, please call me on it."

••

Dan defines culture as values plus behavior. Values should remain constant, but appropriate behavior will change as a company grows. A decision-making process that works perfectly for five people in a small company will fail miserably for a company of ten thousand. The processes and rules needed to run a company of ten thousand would crush a start-up.

Employees who like NetApp's culture often ask, "How can we make sure the culture doesn't change?" That's the wrong question. Culture *should* change. Think of a child. At seventeen months, she drools, stumbles, and falls down. How cute! But think of the same behavior at seventeen years. Is she raiding the liquor cabinet? You don't want your kid to stay the same, but you do want her to be the best she can be for her stage of growth.

Company culture is exactly the same. It needs to be different depending on the size of the company, its growth rate, the challenges it faces—but always you want the culture and the behaviors to reflect the core values. Examples will be more useful than further philosophizing.

••

Start-ups in the dot-com era had a tricky scheme for buying equipment. The start-up would sell pre-IPO stock to a large vendor, and then use the cash to buy equipment from the same vendor. In the short term, it looked like a win-win deal for everyone. The big company got immediate revenue and the dot-com got valuable equipment for what was often worthless stock. But the whole thing smelled fishy to Dan and Tom. If NetApp had to give the customer money before the customer could afford to buy our product, it was not a real deal.

Tom sent voice mail to all of our salespeople saying, "Your job is to find people who *have* money and sell them something."

Some people felt that we were too squeaky-clean, and that we missed opportunities to cash in on the boom, but really, we dodged a bullet. Companies that bought the worthless stock got into big trouble when they had to write off all those "investments" that vaporized in the crash. Values are often that way. In the short term, they can be frustrating, but in the long term, they keep you out of trouble.

In the mid-1990s, we were competing against our old nemesis, Auspex, for business at the National Security Agency (NSA), the folks who monitor electronic communications around the world. The NSA wanted a feature that neither of us had, but they said they'd buy right away if we would commit to deliver within a year. We knew it would take us at least eighteen months, but Auspex promised that they could meet the target.

Auspex was lying. We had worked there and knew their engineering process well. We believed it would take Auspex even longer than us. At a meeting to decide what to do, we started wondering, should we also lie to the customer? That would actually help them, we reasoned, because then they could choose us and get the feature sooner. We went on in that vein for a while, until one employee said, "I can't believe we're talking about whether to lie to a customer. What's the point of all our values talk if we ignore it? This feels wrong."

I'm not proud to have been part of that discussion. It was wrong. But I am proud that an employee could use our values to shut it down. It made me think back to the question that Florence had asked: How are these values going to be used against us? I now believe that values are best when employees can use them against management. Managers have plenty of ways to punish employees—bad performance reviews, poor raises or no raises at all, demotions, dull work assignments, firings—they don't really need one more. But if a boss says, "Here is what I believe," and means it, that gives employees a tool to fight back. The analogy between a company's values and a country's constitution is apt: a constitution—when it's working right—protects the people from their leaders, not the other way around.

We were honest with the NSA. We told them when we could deliver, even though it wasn't what they wanted to hear. Auspex lied and got the business. Values can be painful.

••

Dan's scars kept him vigilant about business practices and loath to see even a hint of anything shady. But he had a company to run and worried that too many rules and procedures would stifle the energetic spirit that fueled our growth.

There were two ways to go. We could be comprehensive-but-bureaucratic or simple-but-vague. Both have advantages. The first approach is similar to IBM's, where a giant book of carefully documented procedures covers every eventuality.

When in doubt, look it up in the book. (Dan started his career at IBM.) The downside is that it's expensive to create and enforce the procedures, and they tend to curtail initiative and reduce productivity. The other method, which we chose, is to make simple guidelines and then trust people. Deal with exceptions as they come up. We wanted to be lightweight and flexible, and if something broke, we would fix it.

When NetApp got big enough to hire its first internal travel agent, the new employee decided to write a company travel policy. It was dozens of pages long and outlined many scenarios for when someone could fly business class, what size car they could rent, what type of hotel they could book, meals they could eat, and how to get managerial approval for all of the above. It was so complex that we had a long discussion in Dan's staff meeting, trying to figure it all out, and whether we agreed. I began to feel that the whole thing was counter-cultural. What happened to simplicity and trust? "Why not," I asked, "just tell everyone that we are a frugal company and people should not spend money foolishly. But they shouldn't show up at a meeting dog tired and jet-lagged just to save a few bucks." The official travel policy became "Use your common sense."

Even today, a decade later, employees can book travel without their manager's approval. If employees feel that they need to travel to get something done, we shouldn't slow them down. There is an important distinction, however, between "no preapproval" and "no oversight." We do keep track of what people do, and sometimes managers need to give lessons about expense control. We've even uncovered cases of fraud. One employee booked flights and sold them for cash. As long as your processes are good enough to catch problems before too long, it is better to suffer an occasional loss than to slow down everyone in the entire company. The phrase "Trust but verify" comes to mind.

••

Brian Pawlowski is a case study in culture. Before joining NetApp, he worked in the network storage group at Sun. In large companies, it can be hard to find motivation. His group was too small to affect Sun's stock price, so Brian decided to focus on a competitor. Auspex had the biggest NFS systems, which pissed him off because Sun had invented NFS. He decided to drive Auspex's stock to zero if he could.

Auspex's key selling point was that their systems were faster than Sun's, so that's where Brian attacked. He fixed every problem he could find. To motivate others to help, he awarded a bottle of good wine to anyone who improved performance by 1 percent. With each bottle, a little piece of Auspex died. One percent sounds small, but big improvements come in small increments, and Brian gave away many cases of wine. A great example of getting things done. Auspex should have offered to pay Brian full-time to go skiing, just to stop his attack. Once Sun's systems outperformed Auspex's, Brian set his sights on NetApp.

Brian already knew about NetApp because he had lost to us during that bake-off at Synopsys. He was in the second team that came in, after the first team failed. Our product, innovation, and performance impressed him. He eventually concluded that it would be more fun to join us than kill us. He joined as employee number eighteen and is now the CTO.

I like to think that I convinced Brian to join NetApp, despite a pay cut, by asking him, "When are you going to go someplace you could really make a difference?" Years later, Brian told me, "I joined NetApp to change the world." To some people, doing work that matters is more important than money.

Characters in the Dungeons and Dragons game are rated in two ways: from lawful (or rule-following) to chaotic, and from good to evil. Brian is chaotic-good. His methods are unpredictable, but the results are positive. He once gave a technical presentation dressed as a Japanese schoolgirl, complete with starched blouse, plaid skirt, and knee-high socks. It might have been politically incorrect, but the audience was riveted, and I think his silliness helped create an environment that was more tolerant of differences. He started a fashion trend among the engineering staff—no mean feat given that fashion and engineering do not normally go hand in hand—of dying hair strange colors. For a while mine was blue, red, and magenta; it took several months to grow out.

Brian's Fashion Trend

I was walking out of a movie theater with my brother and saw a man with a leather jacket and a purple Mohawk walking toward us. I was trying not to stare, but he seemed to notice anyway, because he was kind of eyeballing me back. As he passed us, he smiled and said, "Dude . . . I work for you." Then he turned a corner and disappeared.

••

Brian Pawlowski was once trying to convince someone to quit his company and come work for us. The guy said, "NetApp sounds interesting but I don't want blue hair or piercings."

"Actually," said Brian, "that's not a requirement."

Brian does extremely well when he has a mission he cares about and is let off the leash to accomplish it. He is a natural leader and motivator. Brian's test for leaders is simple: "Look behind you. If nobody is following, then you aren't one."

After a few years with NetApp, he decided he wanted to move to Australia. He had recently visited the country and liked it, and the idea of conquering an entire continent appealed to him. He went to Dan to ask if he could work down under as a sales engineer. Dan said no: our Australian business was too small. But if Brian wanted to move to Japan, he could work the entire Pacific Rim, including Australia. There was one caveat, however. Brian must dye his hair "back to a color found in nature." It didn't have to be his own color, but it had to look human. Brian's hair at the time was, I believe, fluorescent pink.

I don't know how many CEOs would allow a senior employee to have pink hair in the first place, much less represent the company overseas. But Dan saw that Brian was too strong a talent to waste on a small market. He not only wanted Brian to be an international representative of the company, he wanted him to handle a more important area. His talents were what we cared about, not—except in front of conservative customers—his hair color. Brian, likewise, did not care about business superficiality like wearing power ties; he just wanted to follow his passions, trust his colleagues, and get things done. So he dyed his hair brown and spent a year in Japan.

••

Effective communication is an important tool for building culture, and Tom Mendoza is one of the best public speakers I've seen. I'm more of a writer myself. It's useful for an executive staff to have people who communicate in different ways, because employees understand in different ways. It is educational to see Tom give the same presentation twice in a row, which happens regularly because we do our quarterly all-hands meetings once at 8:30 A.M. for early birds, and once at 10:00 A.M. for engineers. In back-to-back speeches about the same topic, he may use completely different words, different stories, and different customer examples, but in a funny way, both talks are identical. They have the same story arc—they take the audience through the same sequence of emotional responses.

Communication was particularly important after the dot-com crash. The day of the layoffs, Tom presented at the company meeting that we held for the survivors.

Pain. He began by talking about what a hard decision it was to do layoffs. It was not something we felt good about, and was even more painful for the people we laid off, many of them our friends.

Acceptance. Tom talked about the factors that forced the decision. Things were bad, and a quick rebound didn't seem likely. He told the story of when we first realized how bad it was getting. At Dan's staff meeting, Rob Salmon, who ran North American sales, said that customers kept cancelling orders after we completed the sale. Rob was really frustrated. Next we discussed a major software purchase that we were about to make. Dan suddenly got cold feet: "Spending that much money right now makes no sense. We have to cancel." Rob put his head in his hands and said, "I bet that's the exact same discussion our customers have just before they cancel on us." We were doing to our vendors what our customers were doing to us. The rest of us groaned. It was like we were doomed.

Hope. Tom's final piece was about why NetApp was still a great place to be. Downturns create opportunity. Smaller companies that survive have the opportunity to come out on top. He didn't make empty promises—no *everything is going to get better just you wait and see*—but he gave people reasons for hope, and asked them to focus on the things that were in our control.

During the Q&A session at the end, an employee asked, "Are we going to have more layoffs?" The answer was, "Our

Little Old Lady

I remember the first shareholders meeting after the stock hit its $6 low. It had recovered to about $12, so it wasn't quite at its worst ever, but the mood in the room was not cheery. Still, Dan gave a good presentation, and then opened the floor for questions.

A small old woman got up, clutching her walker, and slowly made her way to the microphone. She said, in a quavering voice, "I was watching the stock ticker a couple months ago. When I saw my beloved NetApp hit $6, I almost fell out of my wheelchair rushing to the phone to call my broker—"

What flashed through my head was, *Oh my God, Grandma sold it all at the bottom.* As if I didn't feel bad enough already.

She continued, "—and I told him to buy as much as we could get our hands on. Mr. Warmenhoven, I've doubled my money since then. Here is my question. Whatever you are doing, are you going to keep doing it?"

After a short silence, as her question sank in, the whole audience started laughing and then clapping. One simple question completely changed the mood of the room. I've always wondered whether she did that on purpose, to stop people from being so grumpy. I suspect it was Tom Mendoza in drag.

goal is not to. That's how we set the number, but . . . it's hard to tell how bad it will get. I hope we don't, I really hope we don't." That wasn't the message people wanted to hear, but they felt better not being lied to. NetApp was later than most companies in doing layoffs—Dan had delayed it as much as possible, perhaps longer than was good for the business—and many employees had friends at other companies who had been laid off after management promised no more layoffs.

Later, a reporter interviewed Tom about company culture during economic downturns. Tom said, "It's no big deal for employees to feel good when the stock price keeps going up, and everybody's making lots of money. That's not good culture, that's just people being happy. The test of a strong culture comes when times are tough. Do your people dig in and find more inside of themselves?"

The reporter, however, was fixated on whether we were still maintaining special benefits and perks, like Ping-Pong tables and free bagels, after the crash. Tom said, "I'm really not a hug-a-tree kind of guy. If your company is augering into the ground, then maybe you shouldn't feel good. Part of good culture is winning or having a plan to become winning." The reporter was missing the point. Ping-Pong tables and massage chairs don't create good culture. A good company may provide those things, but that's a symptom of good culture, not a cause of it.

••

Motivated employees who care about their company's goals aren't 10 percent or 20 percent more productive; they can do ten times more. It isn't just the hours they work, although people certainly do work more when they care about what they do, but they are also more effective. Motivation matters.

Motivation is about more than money. Relying solely on paychecks and bonuses is a common mistake, especially in old and established firms. Sixty years ago, Abraham Maslow outlined a hierarchy of needs that all people pursue. The lowest needs are physical—air, water, food. Above those are needs like housing and a job. Maslow's observation is that needs at the bottom of the hierarchy are the most important, but only until they are met. Then a higher need takes priority. When you are gasping for breath, you don't care about finding a new house. At the top of the hierarchy are *self-actualization* and *transcendence*—about making the most of your abilities and making a difference in the world.

In the business world, I interpret Maslow's hierarchy to mean that some motivational tools are more powerful than money. At low salary levels, people may be worried about putting food on the table, buying a car, or finding a place to live, but most employees in high-tech companies have achieved those goals. They may want a nicer car and a bigger house, but upgrading is less motivating than attaining something higher in the hierarchy.

Honesty compels me to admit that I made lots of money when NetApp went public, and being rich is pretty nice. So, I do understand that money is a powerful motivator and should be part of the package. My point is that helping employees use their skills effectively and helping them understand how their work is making a difference in the world is *also* important, especially after they have satisfied their basic needs. Start-ups are attractive to many people because it is so clear that their actions matter. In a small business, the inaction of a single employee can literally kill the company.

••

Tom and I were chatting about a former employee who was a bad culture fit. Tom commented, "Acting the way he did may work in the short run, but over time he just pissed everyone off. He should have understood that life is a long game."

Tom had intuitively captured the essence of some complex game theory. Early game theorists struggled to understand why cooperation exists. Their math seemed to prove that cheating is the best strategy even though they believed that cooperation is sometimes better. Using computer simulations, professor Robert Axelrod found that cheating can work in short games, but in long games where the same players interact over and over, players do best if they cooperate. (For details, see his book, *The Evolution of Cooperation*.)

Tom is not a mathematician or a game theorist—in fact he can barely operate his wristwatch—but he captured some groundbreaking game theory in a simple phrase. In this particular case, Tom's long-life analysis was slightly flawed: the ex-employee was soon found dead in a hotel room next to bags of heroin and cocaine. Never mind the details—Tom's strength is understanding the big picture.

I believe this simple insight—*life is a long game*—explains why values work. In the short run, values often feel painful, but they encourage you to act in ways that work out better in the long run. If you plan to keep selling to the same customers, working with the same people, or living in the same neighborhood, then practicing good values is actually in your own self-interest. Experience has taught me this.

We were honest with the NSA and lost a sale. Two years later, Auspex had still not delivered, and the NSA threw them out. NetApp has now been working with the NSA for over a decade. Auspex is bankrupt. A long game, indeed.

INTERLUDE
Lawyers Aren't Evil—Fairness and Morality Are Not Their Job

When I was young and naive, I thought the justice system was about fairness and morality.

My first exposure to the opposing view was when several college friends became lawyers. They were taught that laws are more like rules of a game. Four of a kind beats a full house, but there's no morality to it. I remember one lawyer arguing that morality and fairness are irrelevant; all that matters is passing some kind of judgment so that people can get on with their lives. This view felt wrong to me, and it helped me understand the reputation that lawyers have for being slimy and evil.

My time at NetApp has resulted in an extensive legal education. An early legal battle with Auspex almost killed us. One time I accidentally violated SEC insider trading rules. Another time I was sued for sexual harassment, violation of the California constitution, and intentional infliction of emotional distress. I wasn't alone. That suit was against all of NetApp's founders, officers, VPs, and board members. It settled out of court, and the alleged harasser no longer works at the company. The lawsuit included the rest of us to get our attention, and it worked! At least two times I've been accused of stealing another company's intellectual property, again along with a long list of people. We didn't do it.

My new slogan: Success breeds litigation.

I have a new respect for the lawyers' point of view. Sometimes what matters most is getting to a conclusion so that everyone can move on.

Suppose you accidentally bought a stolen TV. Let's say you bought it at a reputable store, so it's not like you went to a bad part of town and got 80 percent off from a guy selling stuff from the back of his van. A year later, the original owner somehow finds you, and he wants his TV. You didn't do anything wrong, so you think the old owner should leave you alone and go hunt down whoever stole it. But he argues that he didn't do anything wrong either, and since the TV was his first, he wants it back.

As a society we need a process to determine who gets the TV so that both sides can move on with their lives. Laws are not necessarily about right and wrong. Laws are simply the operating system of the country.

That's all fine for this example, where neither person did anything wrong, but what if your moral intuition says one person was good and the other person evil. Then shouldn't you worry about right and wrong? The lawyer's response is, "That's not my job. Congress passes the laws. As a lawyer, I only care what the law actually says."

To put it in computer terms, Congress is the programmer, laws are the program, and the courtroom—lawyers, judge, and jury—are the computer that runs the program. Blame Microsoft for that blue screen, not Dell. This analogy convinced me that the problem is Congress and not the lawyers.

Still, I think it's wrong if *nobody* worries about "moral bugs" in the legal code. It may not be the lawyer's job, but if the legal system veers too far from people's moral intuition, then society runs into trouble. Perhaps we have too many ex-lawyers in Congress. As lawyers they could legitimately ignore the moral implications of laws, but that left them ill prepared for the moral debugging that ought to be part of their job in Congress.

There is also an important lesson for companies: The law sometimes matters less than the judgment of the public. Even if a company follows the strict letter of the law, it will run into trouble if it violates the moral intuition of its customers, shareholders, and employees. Saying "What I did was legal" is often a bad defense.

6

MANAGING ENGINEERS

On Development, Consensus,
Doctor Death, and Magic

I thought Dan was crazy when he asked me to run the engineering department. It was 250 people, and my only previous management experience was when a couple of engineers reported to me for three months, after which we mutually agreed that it would be best for all involved to end the experiment. If I couldn't manage 2, what made Dan think I could manage 250? His argument was this: "Managing a big group is nothing like managing a handful of people. As a low-level manager, you work closely with the group and what they are doing. When you're managing 250 people, you have 5 people reporting directly to you, and they each have 50 people under them. You can't just tell the 5 what to do because they have to turn around and give direction to their 50. Instead, you describe your vision. You help them understand where you want to go, and share any thoughts you have on how to get there. Then trust them." He said that figuring out the big picture and communicating it to people was what I did anyway, so how hard could it be?

It's a good lesson in CEO thinking to understand why Dan thought this made sense. He had four main requirements for a VP of engineering: he wanted someone who understood our technology; he wanted someone who understood our market and customers; he wanted someone who fit NetApp's culture; and finally, he wanted someone with good management experience. I had no management experience, but he argued that nobody would meet all four requirements. Our technology and our market were so new that we probably couldn't find an outsider who was familiar with them. I met three of the four, and he said he'd rather take a risk on me than on some new person he didn't know. Dan's bet was that I could learn, and if not, he could always fire me.

Understanding CEOs

A young engineer was leaving the office at 7 P.M. when he found the CEO standing in front of a paper shredder with a document in his hand. "Listen," said the CEO, "this is important, and my secretary has left. Can you make this thing work?"

"Certainly," said the young engineer. He turned the machine on, inserted the paper, and pressed the start button. "Excellent, excellent!" said the CEO as his paper disappeared inside the machine. "I only need one copy."

I took the job. (Maybe this time I would be the bull.)

••

My predecessor was Helen Bradley, one of the VPs that Dan hired in 1995 to prepare for going public. She had told him that she would take the job for four years, and it turned out she meant exactly four years, so in 1999, Dan needed a new VP. Helen grew engineering from 16 people to

250—four doublings in four years. She knew she'd be retiring, even though Dan didn't believe her, so she put a structure in place that practically ran itself. It was the perfect environment for a neophyte boss like me.

Helen taught me that you can apply engineering-style thinking to the problems of management. Helen had been a programmer, and she said, "Now that I'm a manager, I program with people." She was designing a department instead of a product, and she worked with people instead of electrical components, but she argued that the principles were the same. I could still think like an engineer even as I transformed into a businessman. I'd still ask "How does it work?" and "What problems might cause failure?" but I was troubleshooting people and processes instead of technology. This approach gave me a leg up on businesspeople who lack an engineering mind-set.

Steve Kleiman, our CTO at the time, had a theory about engineers and managers. He divided the world into people who have technical orgasms and people who have management orgasms, or TOs and MOs for short. A TO is when an engineer says, "What if we store the data in NV-RAM and not do the file allocation until later? By delaying that processing we'll speed up the packet response time to the network and get better block layout optimization on the disk drive. . . . Whee!" Engineers are technology-centric. They focus on how things work, on what new technologies are available to solve problems, and on how old technologies are breaking down.

In the beginning, the nerds ran engineering. We needed some MOs to counterbalance all of the TOs. A management orgasm is when a manager says, "I set up this team and coached the leader on how to hire good people and manage them effectively, and now he's matured to the point that he can start other teams and coach their managers, so I have more time to focus on the annual budget and planning process. . . . Whee!" Management-centric thinking is about resources and processes—the people, dollars, labs, schedules, procedures, and action items required to complete a product on budget and on time.

Helen designed an organization that paired managers with senior engineers. The manager of a ten-person group would have a senior engineer to guide the technical direction of the group. More senior managers would have more senior engineers in a parallel structure all the way up to the top—the VP of engineering was paired with the CTO. Some people can do both styles of thinking, but they are rare. What's more, both roles are full-time jobs. Steve was always very skeptical of people who wanted to be managers but also keep doing hands-on engineering.

Here is an example of how good engineers think. Tape drives used to be much cheaper than disk drives, which is why people used tapes for backups—copies made in case something bad happens to the original. Every year disks and tapes were both getting less expensive, but Steve noticed that disk prices were dropping much faster. He predicted that disks would eventually become cheaper than tapes—or so close that it didn't matter. This was years ago, and today NetApp makes hundreds of millions of dollars a year helping customers do backups with disk instead of tape. Steve is always on the lookout for this sort of change, where something that has been true for years (tapes are way cheaper) becomes false. In technology as in business, change creates opportunity.

A friend of mine ran a two-day conference for hundreds of engineers, and afterward she asked several attendees for feedback. Some of the criticism she got surprised her. One engineer complained that the lunch line would have moved faster if it had gone down *both* sides of the buffet table. "Were they even paying attention to the presentations that were the actual point of the conference?" she asked me. I tried to reassure her: "You don't understand how engineers think. We spot problems and try to fix them. If the layout of the food line was the worst problem they found to work on, then you had a spectacular meeting."

••

After taking over from Helen, I realized that we were missing a third style of thinking. Customer-centric thinking is the ability to identify customer pain and figure out what it takes to relieve it. At first, James and I and the other engineers had great intuition about our customers, because we were designing products for people much like ourselves—small groups of engineers doing hardware and software development. Our intuition broke down as we broadened our customer base to include banks, government agencies, and other people who

> ### Understanding Engineers
>
> The pessimist sees the glass as half empty. The optimist sees the glass as half full. The engineer says, "This glass is twice as big as it needs to be."
>
> ••
>
> Q: What's the difference between an introverted engineer and an extroverted engineer?
>
> A: The extroverted engineer looks at *your* shoes when he talks to you.

were very different from us. Groups that specialize in this type of thinking are often called *product marketing* or *product management*. Their goal is to find problems that customers will pay money to fix.

Leaving out customer-centric thinking is a common flaw in organizational design. Everyone knows that you need engineers to develop a new product, so it's unlikely you'd forget about them, although some companies don't include technology-centric thinking in the decision-making process as much as they should. And after you've hired five or ten engineers, you are probably going to want a manager for them to report to, so hopefully you'll find a good one and get management-centric thinking. But engineers and managers sometimes assume that if they build a technically elegant product and ship it on time, then customers will naturally want to buy it. Not true.

If a team is missing any of these three thinking styles, you get pathological results. Here's an example. A product manager goes up to an engineer and says, "We're going to sell this great new product. It's wallpaper. Right now, wallpaper is annoying to install. It's always wrinkling and the glue gets all over. But not our new wallpaper. You put it up against the wall and it fits itself perfectly to the right spot before sticking. No wrinkles, no cutting, and no glue. This will make us millions."

The engineer gets excited and says, "That sounds great. How does it work?"

The product manager says, "That's your job."

If you are missing technology-centric thinking, as in this story, you get a great idea for a product that customers would love to buy, except there's no way to actually build it.

On the other hand, if you are missing customer-centric thinking, you get an elegant design that works great and ships on time, except customers don't care very much about the problem it solves. They might admire it as a technical achievement, but they won't buy it. Tom Mendoza put it best: "Customers don't open their wallets unless they are feeling pain."

Venture capitalists often think in terms of the same three areas when deciding whether to fund companies. They argue about whether it is the technology that is more important, the managerial skill and experience, or the market opportunity, but in the end they recognize that all three are critical. In the case of NetApp, I think the VCs recognized our technical skill, but they didn't think we had enough management experience or a good understanding of our target market.

Thinking about organizations this way is a great example of management-centric thinking. For a manager assembling a team, it's important to make sure that you have all three thinking styles represented in your group. Even for nonmanagers, I would argue that it's useful to understand this model so you can tell if you are in a healthy team. Understanding the different styles of thinking can help you value them. Don't hate people for being different—rely on them for their special skill. Finally, figuring out which style you love is critical to choosing a satisfying career path.

••

When I became VP of engineering, I often went to Tom for management advice. He always asked about the people working on the problem: Who was involved? What else were they working on? What were they good at?

Tom thought very differently from me. I would dig into the problem itself: I'd learn about the details, explore the options, and worry about the right answer. Tom didn't focus on the problem: he focused on the people whose job was to solve the problem. After talking with Tom, I seldom understood the problem any better, but he gave me lots of ideas about how to move forward in solving it. Occasionally I was the right person to come up with a solution, but as the organization grew, it became obvious to me that Tom's approach was much more powerful and scalable. Watching Tom manage, it seemed to me that he applied a simple three-step algorithm to every problem:

1. Who owns the problem?
2. Do I trust them?
3. How do I find an owner I trust?

If you can't find an owner, that's the problem right there. Skip to step 3. Sometimes it's obvious what person or group owns the problem, but they need to be reminded that it's theirs and that you are watching.

When you find the owner, the next step is to figure out whether you trust them. I don't mean trust in some abstract sense—I mean trust them to fix this particular problem. In the abstract, I trust Tom Mendoza completely. For a problem involving spreadsheets or programming languages, not at all. Even if you trust someone's skills, that person may be too busy to do more. You're looking for someone with the skills, the time, and the passion to solve this problem.

If steps 1 and 2 fail, then step 3 is to find an owner you trust. Sometimes there's someone nearby who can take it on.

Other times you may need to reassign someone or hire a new person. When you're a manager, the answer is sometimes *do it yourself*, but the larger your organization, the less often this is true.

Tom's background is sales, and he knows absolutely nothing about programming, so imagine my surprise when he used the programming technique of recursion. By following steps 1 and 2 he concluded that he needed to hire someone to own a particular problem. *Hire someone* became the new problem, and by following steps 1 and 2 he concluded that he wanted to use an external headhunter. *Find a headhunter* became the new problem, and—here we reach the root of the recursion—Tom identified the owner as the VP of human resources, someone he trusted to find the headhunter to hire the employee to solve the problem. Problem solved.

••

Cooperation, collaboration, and consensus are part of NetApp's culture. We feel that they make for a better work environment, better decisions, and better alignment. However, consensus can lead to paralysis if carried too far. Simply giving one person ownership for a decision—saying, "You can do whatever you want!"—would certainly be much faster. How do you balance between these two extremes? What does it mean to be the owner of a decision?

My team and I were struggling with these issues, and I asked Dan for his advice on what it means to delegate the ownership of a decision to someone. He said: "When I delegate, I want the owner to identify the key stakeholders and bring them to a consensus on the right plan. If they fail, then the decision comes back to my staff meeting, preferably in the form of different recommendations to choose from. I am sometimes a key stakeholder, so don't forget about me when driving to consensus."

The trickiest issue was defining *consensus*. Even when people have a rough agreement, they may differ on details. Does consensus mean 100 percent agreement? If not, who determines whether consensus has been reached? What does it mean to own a decision if you still have to reach consensus?

I asked Dan all these questions, and he said: "If the owner and key stakeholders cannot reach agreement, then I will decide, or maybe send them back to try again. But everyone should be aware that I have a strong bias to accept the owner's recommendation. Consensus doesn't mean that you agree 100 percent with the owner. Withholding consent means that you believe the owner's plan is fundamentally broken, and you want to try to convince me of that, despite my bias to accept the owner's recommendation. I am not interested in arguments about the owner's plan is good, but mine is better. I won't judge beauty contests. Go convince the owner. But if a plan is really busted, please do tell me about that!"

I love this definition of consensus because it is pragmatic, not philosophical theory. If you are a stakeholder trying to decide whether to withhold consent, consider whether the owner's case is really so weak that you can overcome Dan's "strong bias" to go with the owner. But if you are an owner, and key stakeholders are objecting, consider whether their case is so weak that Dan will ignore it. Maybe you should work harder to accommodate the stakeholders' concern and reach consensus. I bet your plan will be stronger for it.

As near as I can tell, this is Dan's ownership model for pretty much everything. I can't think of many times that Dan has told the owner, "You can do whatever you want, and I'll support it." On the other hand, for many areas it is very clear who the owner is, and unless people can point to a serious, serious problem with the owner's plan, they are unlikely to withhold consent.

••

Being new to management, I worked with a management coach, which I recommend strongly, if you can find the right one. Isabella Conti was my coach, and when she polled my staff, their biggest complaint was that I made decisions too slowly. Perhaps I was reacting against my experience with Mike Malcolm, who I thought made decisions too fast and too often. Part of my problem was that I don't really like telling people what to do: I prefer for a group consensus to emerge. Unfortunately, consensus is sometimes slow and painful. The message from my group was that some decisions aren't important enough to bother with consensus. Should staff meetings be on Tuesday or Wednesday? Either way you'll inconvenience somebody, but it's not that big a deal. The boss should just decide and save time for everyone. Other decisions may be important enough for consensus, but—for whatever reason—consensus is never going to happen. Maybe different people have strongly held beliefs and they aren't changing. Again, the boss should decide—perhaps after some attempt at consensus—and save time for everyone.

Managers have a range of decision-making options. They can decide by themselves, decide with group input, delegate to one owner, seek group consensus, or even seek unanimous agreement. The trick is to use all the styles, as appropriate, and not just one. My coach suggested that we have a decision drive. Everyone on my staff could list up to five decisions that were festering, and my homework assignment was to respond to all of them. I didn't have to decide them myself, but the assignment was that for each one, I needed a process to close the decision in relatively short order. Dealing with such a big list at once forced me to use a variety of techniques, and we cleared up the backlog.

In this particular case, Dan's advice was not so useful. He said, "Never make a decision before you have to." That's probably good advice for someone, but not for me. Advice is funny that way: what's perfect for one person may be awful for another.

My coach's advice went from subtle, like the decision drive, to simple. I sometimes struggled to escape from one-on-one meetings that were running over. Little hints didn't always work. Isabella's simple advice: "Stand up. Then they'll stand up—it's only natural. And then you can both walk toward the door."

I remembered some other management lessons from my life before NetApp. Bill Horton, a director back when I was at Auspex, taught me the importance of early milestones. It's common to throw a party when a product finally ships, but that's not very motivational because by then the engineers who did initial design work may have already moved on to other projects. So Bill looked for things to celebrate early in the development process. The instant we met the goal, he would make a big announcement and open a bottle of champagne, whatever time it was.

They say with dogs that you cannot punish them three days later for crapping on the floor. You have to drag them over and rub their noses in it right away. Bill applied the same principle, except he rubbed our noses in success.

Bill also used the milestones to bring teams together. Sometimes a big project has separate groups working on separate components, and they don't connect them up until the very end. Bill would set a goal that required the parts to work together. That often exposed problems that would have been much harder to fix later on. At NetApp, I encouraged managers to set creative early milestones and keep a bottle of champagne on hand.

••

Sometimes alcohol is the reward for teamwork, and sometimes it is the inspiration.

"What would you like to drink?" the flight attendant asked.

I was on a business trip with a coworker named Laura Pickering, and we must have been thirsty because we answered together. "Cranberry and—" said Laura. "Dr Pepper," I interrupted. "—vodka," Laura finished. Laura wanted a Sea Breeze (cranberry and vodka), and I wanted Dr Pepper, but since we interrupted each other, the flight attendant got confused.

"You want cranberry, *Dr Pepper*, and vodka?!"

Seizing the moment, Laura said, "Huh? Uh, sure, I'll take one."

"Make that two," I added.

We had accidentally invented a new drink that we christened Doctor Death. We named it after we'd each had two more. The recipe is one-third cranberry, one-third Dr Pepper, and one-third vodka. It's better than you might expect. The sourness of the cranberry cuts the sweetness of the Dr Pepper, and together they hide the alcohol, giving the drink a dangerous kick like a Long Island Iced Tea. Hence the death in the name. The Doctor Death story is my favorite metaphor for collaboration, because it neatly captures something that I've seen often in brainstorming meetings.

Here's the key question: Who invented the Doctor Death?

I guess you could say it was Laura and me, because we requested it, even though we didn't intend to. Or maybe it was the flight attendant when she repeated back what she thought she had heard, even though she got it wrong. Or perhaps the magic point of invention was when Laura decided to try this new drink, even though the whole thing was a mistake. Or maybe it was when I ratified her choice by ordering the second Doctor Death in the history of the world. In the end, I conclude that it was a group effort. None of the individuals involved would have come up with it on their own.

Cut to the brainstorming meeting. A group of people are working to solve a problem, and together they invent a new solution, but if you try to determine who actually made the invention, it's impossible. One person suggests a solution that isn't quite right, but another person mishears it and repeats it back slightly modified, and the first person says, "That's not what I meant," but a third person says, "You know, that could work!"

In cases like this, it's useless to fight over credit. The result truly is a team effort that can only occur when people are comfortable enough to throw out half-baked ideas and open enough to hear a possible solution even in a mistake or a misinterpretation.

I've seen this many times, and now I have a name for it: Hey, a Doctor Death moment!

••

I am analytic by nature and an engineer by training. I look for "hard" explanations, for cause and effect. "Soft" thinking and mystical new-age hand waving annoy me. So it came as some surprise for me to realize that I believe in magic.

Watching NetApp double is what convinced me. In our last year of growth before the tech crash, we went from about 1,200 employees to over 2,400. The 1,200 new people combined with the existing 1,200 to become a productive team. No single person understood the whole picture, and yet somehow—as if by magic—it worked. Engineering, which I ran, reached 750 people, and I certainly didn't understand it all.

I struggled to reconcile this apparent magic with my pragmatic philosophy until I realized that Arthur C. Clarke, the science fiction writer, had the best explanation. He wrote that any sufficiently advanced technology is indistinguishable from magic. To a primitive tribe on an undiscovered desert island, my flashlight would be magic.

My point is that the human brain is a sufficiently advanced technology. The human mind is far beyond what we can understand and quantify and far beyond what today's computers can do. The best artificial intelligence (AI) systems barely recognize human speech, much less understand it. AI designers recently got excited because a robotic car crossed fifty miles of empty desert, never mind navigating a busy freeway.

If you don't believe in magic, think back to the best boss you ever had, or maybe the best teacher, and I bet you come up with some examples. You can't explain exactly why, but something they said or did motivated you to accomplish more than you thought possible. Maybe pixie dust is the ability to inspire people this way.

The greatest magic is not one human mind; it is multiple minds working together. If we don't understand one by itself, how could we hope to understand a group of them interacting? The magic is most potent of all when the brains are highly motivated and working toward a common goal. I've watched teams made up of hundreds of unmotivated people produce nothing, and I've watched small but motivated teams change a whole industry.

Anthropologist Margaret Mead was on to something when she said, "Never doubt that a small, dedicated group of people can change the world. Indeed, it is the only thing that ever has."

INTERLUDE
Scientific-Truth and Useful-Truth

Sometimes I like to play with ideas. Lately I've been mulling over the distinction between scientific-truth and useful-truth.

Scientific-truth: I believe that the universe is an understandable place, with objective facts that we can discover by using the scientific method.

Useful-truth: I believe that individuals are sometimes better off believing things that may not be scientifically true. What if believing in God makes people happier and more successful, independent of whether God actually exists? In this case, believing in God would be a useful-truth, whether or not it is a scientific-truth.

Suppose that we could find a useful-truth that is scientifically false. Should we believe it? An idea like this would be like magic, because scientifically we know it isn't true, but believing it makes our life better anyway. Any science involving human thoughts and ideas is difficult, but for the sake of argument, let's suppose that we could scientifically prove that this scientific-falsehood was a useful-truth. That would create a paradox: many assume that the scientific method produces the most valid truths, but in this situation, science itself would be showing that it is best to believe a scientific-falsehood.

We might hope that for every useful-truth, there is a scientific argument explaining why it is useful. Then, instead of believing the useful-truth, we could believe the science behind it. This could work if human brains were infinitely powerful computers, but they are not. A simple useful-truth may have a beneficial effect that a much more complex scientific-truth would not. Consider a person in a deadly fight with one chance in a hundred of survival. Believing that I will live if I try hard enough is more likely to inspire the necessary effort than believing that I should try even though I'm 99 percent likely to die. If people's brains were perfect calculating machines, the beliefs might be equal, but they're not equal for the flawed brains we actually have.

What does it mean to be a scientist if science itself is telling you to believe falsehoods? A scientist who abandons scientific-truth to believe useful-truth is no longer practicing science. How does this affect the rest of that scientist's work? If the useful-truth is in an area unrelated to the science, this is no problem, but what about scientific study of useful-truths themselves?

Many scientists believe that scientific-truth is always useful, or at worst neutral. They argue that the problem is in how science is applied, not in science itself. Yet this trust in the value of science is not a scientific-truth. The evidence is quite strong that science is good at producing scientific-truths—facts about the physical world and even facts about the human world—but there is much less evidence that scientific-truths are always useful-truths. I think that scientists and engineers are sometimes offensive because we insist on spouting scientific-truths that are not useful-truths, and this upsets people.

The question of whether different groups of people have equal intelligence is an emotionally charged example. Hypothetically, suppose that on average, left-handers are one IQ point smarter than right-handers. It still wouldn't make sense to assume that the southpaw in a group is the smartest person because the variations between people are so large. Most people are so bad at interpreting scientific and mathematical data that it might be healthier to believe the useful-truth that all people are equal rather than the (hypothetical) scientific-truth that left-handers are one IQ point smarter with a standard deviation of 20. This is a real-world issue because there are hints of differences between groups: women—on average—seem to have stronger language skills; left-handedness may correlate with certain kinds of creativity. Personally, though, I doubt that the effects are strong enough for us to ever predict much about intelligence just by knowing that a person is left-handed and has brown hair.

Maybe we should keep looking for scientific-truths that are just as convincing as important useful-truths. Perhaps we could even discover a scientific-religion. If you believe that religions offer useful-truths that are not scientific-truths, then the trick would be to find the corresponding scientific-truths. You might supplement *God says be nice to your neighbors* with *Axelrod's computer simulations prove that you should be nice to your neighbors.*

I have wandered far into the clouds. Here's some simple advice that is closer to the ground but still related. Armen Varteressian, who was on my staff for many years, told me, "Dave, your job as a vice president is to oversimplify. But be careful that you don't *over*-oversimplify." Here's how I interpret this lesson: If the real truth is too complex to be inspirational, try simplifying it a bit (oversimplify). With luck, you may create a useful-truth. But if you go too far, you might turn it into a disillusioning falsehood (don't over-oversimplify).

PART THREE

..

GROWN-UP COMPANY

Two books deeply influenced my strategic thinking about how companies mature: *The Innovator's Dilemma*, by Clayton Christensen, and *Inside the Tornado*, by Geoffrey Moore. You should still read them, even though I share some key lessons here.

The Innovator's Dilemma was a revelation to me because it so clearly explained strategic issues that we faced at NetApp. The book explores the observation that low-end technologies tend to move upmarket and outperform high-end technologies. Mainframes were the original high-end computer: very large, fast, and reliable, but also very expensive. At first, UNIX was for desktop workstations, but over time computers running UNIX replaced mainframes in many large companies. Then Microsoft Windows started replacing UNIX, and now Linux may replace them both. This keeps happening: small new computers replace big old computers. (In twenty years, major corporations may run their billing systems on smart phones.)

The key is that technology gets better, according to Christensen, faster than customer requirements go up. In many markets, things get better and cheaper at the same time. Laptops are a great example. Ten years ago, my laptop was much slower than my desktop. Today, my laptop is so fast that I don't need a separate desktop. If a vendor offered me a laptop that was twice as fast, I would say, "I'd rather have the same speed at half the price. Why not make it lighter? Or make the batteries last longer. And while you're at it, make it cooler so my lap doesn't get so hot." Laptop performance is improving much faster than my needs are increasing. When customers no longer care whether a particular aspect of a product gets any better, Christensen calls it a *goodness oversupply*. (I love that concept!) There's nothing wrong with a goodness oversupply, but people won't pay extra for it.

A second point in the book is that two parallel markets often focus on roughly the same problem, one for high-end customers and the other for low-end customers. A good example from outside the high-tech world is the personal music market, with the living room stereo and the iPod. Often the low-end product has other advantages besides cost. The iPod fits in my pocket, so for portable music, it's much better. Buying music is easier too because I can download it online.

As low-end products improve, they eventually get good enough to satisfy the market above them, and they have advantages that help them win. Not only are they cheaper, but because they are designed for less sophisticated users, they are simpler to use. Since they aim at a larger market, they often have higher unit volumes, which drives costs down even more. They may have other advantages besides, as with the iPod. All this makes it very difficult for the high-end vendors to defend themselves.

Christensen's theories helped me understand how NetApp and NAS could win against larger and more entrenched competitors, first against Auspex, and later against major IT vendors like IBM, HP, and EMC. NetApp's NAS started as a low-end technology that was only good enough for small workgroups. Our competitors sold a different type of storage called SAN, which was—at first—faster and more reliable, but also much more expensive and harder to manage. As NAS improved over time, we found ourselves competing against SAN and winning.

••

Inside the Tornado describes different stages of technology adoption, from the early adopters who will try any crazy new technology to the quill-pen crowd who stick to the previous generation of technology as long as possible. Moore has lots of detailed advice for each stage, but for me, the most important lesson is that a company must periodically make 180-degree flips in its strategy. For instance, he argues that it is appropriate for early stage start-ups to invent technologies that can solve many different problems for many different people, because such broad solutions have enormous potential. And yet, when it comes time to establish a sales footprint and get profitable, Moore argues that it's critical to solve a particular problem for a particular type of customer: Put all your eggs in one basket, and watch that basket closely.

Suppose you have five potential problems you could solve, and your product is 40 percent good enough for all of them. If you invest in all five areas, you might get them each to 50 percent good enough, which still won't make anyone happy. Much better to invest in just one—the trick is to choose the right one—and take it to 80 or 90 percent. Don't start investing in a second problem area until you've got a solid and successful solution for the first one.

Notice how the strategy keeps flipping, from broad to narrow to broad. As an early start-up, you think broadly about what problems you can solve. After you've gained experience with some early customers, you choose just one group to focus on—a very narrow strategy. After you've succeeded there and have more resources to invest, you broaden out again.

"Don't cross the street by yourself," you tell your four-year-old son, but a few years later you say, "It's okay to cross the street by yourself." It's not that the early strategy was wrong and then you fixed it; the point is that different stages of development require different strategies, and often the appropriate strategy at one stage is the opposite of the strategy for the previous stage.

This recognition is important when it's time to drive change through an organization. People often resist change, and I think part of the resistance comes from a feeling that if it's necessary to do something different, then they must have been doing something wrong before. People don't like to admit that they were wrong. Never mind worrying whether things were all screwed up before—it's much healthier to focus on what strategy is best for now.

7

CUSTOMERS

On Love, Enterprise, Simplicity, and Partners

Tom Mendoza shredded our initial sales strategy as soon as we hired him. To grow a business, you must find either more customers or bigger customers. Our original plan was to sell to start-ups, or to small engineering workgroups within large companies, and find lots of them. Instead of selling to ten small companies, Tom asked, why not sell ten times as much— or a hundred times—to one large company? Once we got in the door, we would be able to count on a regular and significant stream of orders rolling in automatically as the customer grew. "We'll make millions," Tom said, "as long as the fax machine doesn't break."

This chapter is the story of how NetApp learned to satisfy the largest corporations in the world and matured into a grown-up company.

In retrospect, it's not surprising that our first customers were engineering workgroups. James and I had spent our entire careers as engineers in Silicon Valley, and as I said in Chapter Six, we designed a product that we would like to use ourselves. This is a common pattern. Sun, in its early days, consisted mostly of hardware and software engineers, and they developed workstations for use by hardware and software engineers. Apple consisted of two home computer hobbyists, and their first product was—surprise!—a home computer for hobbyists. We have met the customers, and they are us. This is a great strategy because you automatically have a strong, intuitive understanding of your customers.

Tom's point was that large engineering groups are very similar to small ones, but they need more storage and have more money. So our first big customer transition was from small engineering workgroups to higher-end technical and scientific computing. We didn't have to change much to reach these new customers. They were still very technical, so the sales process was similar: we would explain how our box worked, why it was better than the competition, and customers would figure out themselves how it could solve their problems. At many companies, we already had a foot in the door. Our storage was cheap enough to fit within the budget of a first-line manager, so rogue engineering groups would buy our storage if they got tired of waiting for someone upstairs to solve their problem. When we started selling at the departmental level, we already had supporters who could act as internal references.

Our products worked for both small and large technical environments. At first the most common applications were software development and chip design. Later we added seismic processing for oil and gas companies. They take multi-terabyte "photographs" of the ground, analyze them like crazy, which produces even more terabytes, and then crunch all that data down to a single bit of information: *drill* or *don't drill*. (To put the amount of data in context, one terabyte would hold about two million copies of this book.) The military intelligence community is similar, except that they take multi-terabyte satellite photographs and crunch them down to a different bit of information: *bomb* or *don't bomb*. Hollywood studios used our equipment to store animated movies like *Ratatouille* and computerized special effects for movies like *King Kong* and *Transformers*.

••

Internet customers became especially important as the dot-com boom progressed. At first they were like other technical customers. System administrators from technology companies started many of the early Internet companies as a hobby, because they wanted to read newsgroups that weren't allowed at work (not only porn, although that was a factor). They installed equipment in the garage and sold login privileges to friends to help cover the costs. They naturally bought equipment that was familiar to them: Sun computers, Cisco routers, and NetApp storage.

The requirements for Internet companies changed dramatically when they realized that shutting down service for thousands (later millions) of people would earn them front page headlines. Suddenly their applications were mission critical— they absolutely had to keep working 100 percent of the time. Often they'd fire their first CEO and hire one with experience making things very reliable, like someone from a telephone company. Even though they were start-ups, they wanted the reliability that was normally associated with mature corporate data centers and they were unhappy if they didn't get it.

I remember a particularly painful meeting with Yahoo in the mid-nineties. Yahoo was one of our largest Internet customers, and they stored all of their e-mail on NetApp. They told us, "We built our entire infrastructure on your equipment. Our customer base is doubling every three months, and your NAS storage has allowed us to scale faster than anything else we can imagine. But if we could find an alternative to NetApp, we would throw you out in an instant."

Their complaint: "You aren't reliable enough." Quality that's great for a department of engineers doesn't cut it for a giant data center supporting millions of customers.

We could have told Yahoo, "We're sorry that you chose to build a high-reliability data center out of workgroup equipment. It's no surprise that it doesn't meet your needs. This must be very difficult for you." Yahoo was frustrated with us, but really it was a tough love message. They hoped NetApp would succeed, because they depended on us to enable their rapid growth. We could have turned them down, but they represented enormous opportunity. Not only was Yahoo a big customer, but we felt that other Internet companies would face the same issues. What's more, we were getting similar complaints from Cisco, which was one of our largest tech customers. They loved our systems at first, but like Yahoo, they started running into reliability problems when they had installed hundreds of them. We decided to focus on Yahoo's and Cisco's needs.

James and I had mostly worked in small companies, and we were clueless about big companies with big data centers. We no longer had an intuitive understanding of our customers' needs. I suppose it's inevitable that the strategy of sticking to what you know breaks down. If you keep growing long enough, you will eventually start selling to customers who are less like yourself. This is when you need to hire people with the customer-centric thinking skills described in Chapter Five. At a start-up serving customers like yourself, you unconsciously do the right thing; to mature that start-up into a large company serving other large companies, you must learn to consciously study and understand their special needs.

Bad Hair Day

I was once on a sales call in New York, talking about NetApp's commitment to product quality. I told a story about how I tried to motivate the engineering department by promising to dye my hair any crazy color they wanted if they could reduce our failure rate by a factor of ten.

The magenta, blue, and red had long since grown out, so the customer looked me over and said, "And they chose gray?"

As VP of engineering, I started a program called "Love Yahoo/Love Cisco." I appointed a full-time chief love officer (CLO), with the job of doing whatever it took to make Yahoo and Cisco happy. The motto was *Customize then Standardize.* If he had to customize our products to meet their needs, then so be it, but I also wanted him to put those changes back into our standard products so that the rest of our customers would eventually get the benefit too. Many salespeople asked me to add their customers to the Love Program, but I always refused. My main goal wasn't to make Yahoo and Cisco happy—although that was a nice side effect—but to *learn from them.* Yahoo was one of our largest and most demanding Internet customers; if we could make Yahoo happy, we could make any Internet company happy. Likewise, for Cisco and other tech companies.

The Love Program completely changed our product road map. We designed systems that worked in pairs—if one failed the other could take over. We wrote software that replicated all data to a remote location—no data loss even if a data center burned down. And lots more technical details I won't get into. We had to cancel or delay many other projects, but Yahoo and Cisco represented so much opportunity that it was worth it.

Investing in the Love Program was a major turning point for the company. Yahoo and Cisco are both still big customers today. If we had not taken their pain seriously, we would have remained a low-end company, and I believe that our growth would have stalled. In essence, we were betting that tech and Internet companies could fuel our growth, and we were right. By the time we reached a billion dollars, 70 percent of our revenue came from those two categories.

••

In betting on Yahoo, we were betting on the Internet. Earlier I said that the Internet was a giant wave that we spotted and chose to ride. The wave eventually crashed, but the ride carried us far. Our improvements in reliability and data protection set the foundation for going after enterprise customers more broadly.

The term *enterprise* refers to large businesses solving large problems. When people talk about *enterprise-class equipment*, they mean equipment reliable enough to handle your most mission-critical applications: stuff that would really damage your business if it failed. Many engineering groups don't qualify as enterprise. For a large group, failure could mean that hundreds of engineers sit idle. It's a big waste of time and—if it happened too often—could hurt the company's competitiveness. But most engineers work on products that won't ship for months or years, so a day or two of downtime can be absorbed in the development schedule. Painful, but it probably doesn't put the company at risk.

To understand enterprise, consider Southwest Airlines. If their storage fails, they can't sell tickets. In this post-9/11 era, if they can't access their passenger lists or cargo manifests, both stored on NetApp, it is illegal for their planes to take off. If the NetApp storage stays down for two hours, then every Southwest plane in the air must land immediately at the nearest airport. It may be painful for Cisco if their development engineers sit idle for a few hours, but that's nothing compared to the pain that Southwest would feel. This is why enterprise customers are so, so conservative. Companies are most protective of the applications with which they collect money from customers, count their money, or provide services to their customers.

Yahoo and other Internet companies were sort of enterprise: they did rely on our storage to provide services to their customers, but being so young and so recently managed like tech startups, they didn't have the justified paranoia of mature enterprise companies. For years, Tom Mendoza tried to get NetApp into Wall Street trading firms. I remember him describing one meeting with a chief information officer (CIO) where she started by saying, "Okay, I know your story. You can do everything EMC can do, and you can do it for a lot less, right?" (EMC was and is our biggest competitor.) Tom nodded, and she said, "With a story like that, you will never make a single sale on Wall Street. My company has plenty of money, and as long as everything keeps working, I'll get promoted. *Why would I change anything?*"

For enterprise customers, change equals risk. Consider the cost of an airline grounding every plane or of a Wall Street firm not being able to execute trades. The downside is so painful that they need a very, very good reason to change. If they have plenty of money and a solution that works, there is almost no amount of savings that would justify a new vendor, and especially not an unknown newcomer. Remember Tom Mendoza's saying: Customers only open their wallets when they are in pain.

Fortunately for us, the tech crash sent the economy south, and the recession was good for us. It created so much pain that conservative enterprise customers were forced to consider new solutions. The attitude changed from, *I'll be promoted if I keep things working* to *I'll be fired if I don't cut costs.* The tech crash also gave us extra incentive to go after the enterprise companies, because our Internet and technology customers—70 percent of our revenue—pretty much stopped buying.

••

We had actually been going after enterprise customers for several years before the crash. Dan was paranoid—in a good way—and relying so much on tech and Internet companies scared him. In the late nineties, Dan decided to target five additional market areas. The first was financial services, which was why Tom kept trying so hard to get into Wall Street, and the others were telecommunications, oil and gas, major manufacturing, and the U.S. government. Today we're a major vendor in all five areas, but early on it was tough going.

I got an early hint that selling to non-tech companies was different when I made a sales call on Georgia Pacific, the paper company. I gave my best presentation about WAFL and RAID and Snapshots—all the NetApp technologies—and speed and reliability, the same tech-laden pitch that worked wonders with engineers. When I finished, the IT manager leaned forward and talked slowly, with a deep southern drawl: "Son. You gotta understand, here at Georgia Pacific, we take trees, and we turn 'em into toilet paper. What you need to explain to me is, exactly how will your box help me to do that?" He was polite about it, but he clearly didn't care at all about our wonderful technology. My reaction at the time was to wonder how a company could survive without a more inquisitive IT department. (We didn't get that sale.)

I got another hint when I visited an insurance company in the Midwest. The IT manager told me, "My strategy here is not to hire smart people." His whole staff was sitting around the table, smiling and nodding. I was stunned! He called his staff idiots, right to their faces, and it didn't bother them. To me, *smart* was the ultimate compliment, but he didn't see it that way. What he was trying to tell me, but I was not yet clever enough to understand, was that he didn't hire people to understand all the technical details of his data center. His strategy was to buy from vendors who could send in people to handle those details for him. His folks were plenty competent, but their skill was in overseeing the work of technology companies, not in understanding the technology itself. I saw smart as a good thing, but to him it meant something more like *troublesome propeller-heads that I'd rather rent than hire*. (We didn't get that sale either.)

Rob Salmon, our then VP of North American sales, described an experience that finally helped me understand what was going on. Rob was going to meet the CIO of one of our first banking customers on the East Coast. Rob checked with our customer support organization before his trip to see if there had been any problems. No failures, just some simple questions, so Rob expected an easy call.

The CIO began the conversation by saying, "Rob, I want you to know that your sales guys really piss me off!" Not what Rob expected, so he asked what we were doing wrong. The CIO said, "Here's the problem. They come in and they tell me all about your products. They tell me how fast they are, they tell me how reliable they are, how they work, speeds and feeds—more technical detail about your products than I could possibly want to know. And then they sit back and smile, like they're done."

"What should they do?" Rob asked.

"I pay you guys enough money that I want you to figure out my problems. I don't want to figure out what your products do. You come in and look around, and you tell me how your products will fix my problems. That's what I want." In retrospect, that was pretty much what the man from Georgia Pacific was trying to explain. If you listen carefully enough, customers will often tell you how to win their business.

NetApp now has many customers who spend millions of dollars a year with us. The largest ones spend around $100 million a year. I don't know if you have ever written a check for $100 million—I personally have not—but if I ever do, I can tell you one thing for sure: My expectations will be quite high. This may be the most important lesson of enterprise selling.

••

Although I started the Love Program in order to improve our products—I was the VP of engineering, after all—it also uncovered many nonproduct issues that helped us with enterprise customers.

An example was the way we handled product failures when we were small. A customer once called late at night with a big problem. An engineer named Varun Mehta, who happened to be working late, took the call and determined that their system needed to be replaced. He couldn't find anyone from customer service, so he went to the manufacturing floor, pulled a new box off the line, and got on a plane to Los Angeles. He rented a van, drove to the customer's site, and worked all night to solve the problem. The next morning, the customer called and told us the story, but when we went to look for Varun to thank him, he wasn't to be found. After hours of searching, we discovered that he had been asleep in the rental van in the customer's parking lot. This small customer saw Varun as a hero, and I felt the same way. He exemplified our values by going beyond the call of duty to make a customer successful.

Large companies have a very different perspective on failure: Heroics scare them. The difference is that small customers, with one or two systems, will probably never see a failure. If something does break, they are thrilled if we can fix it quickly. Large customers buy so many systems that things will break periodically no matter how high the reliability. Part of our problem with Cisco and Yahoo was that we needed more reliable systems, but we also needed to offer a better *failure experience*.

Much of the failure experience comes from how people in the company behave. Are there repeatable processes to handle failure, staffed with full-time people who understand how customers think? Heroics scare large customers because heroes come and go. They want to know that you'll handle the problem the same way, the right way, every time. They certainly don't want Varun sleeping in a van in their parking lot.

This is a great example of how behaviors need to change even as values stay the same. I want our employees today to work just as hard as Varun did to ensure customer success, but I also hope that no engineer ever again sneaks into manufacturing at midnight and swipes a replacement system. We do it differently now.

Years later I got a lesson on failure experience from a support engineer in our call center. Walking by his cube, I noticed that he had ripped dozens of pages out of the manual and taped them on the wall. I figured he might have some good ideas for improving the product, so I gestured to the wall and asked, "What is most important when a customer calls?" He said, "The most important thing is that they don't hear me flipping through a manual."

Semper Wi Fi

We invited customers to a meeting to share their storage experiences, and several military officers came. The military uses a bunch of our equipment, some in Iraq bolted inside Humvees. Combat generates lots of data.

One officer mentioned the *smoking pit scenario,* and a civilian in the room asked, "What's that?" The officer explained, "Our mission is to support the warfighter no matter what, even if a data center is bombed and becomes a smoking pit."

Later a civilian described the work he was doing to create a secure data center, and the same officer said, "People like to think all strategic, but sometimes you've got to be more tactical. Like if you're out in the field, and you need a secure data center, I say put up a tent and two marines in front with .45s. There is your secure data center."

I was being technology-centric, but he was focused on the customer. The sound of frantic page turning does not inspire confidence.

••

Our philosophy was to build products with appliance-like simplicity. But was simple always better? There is a tension between a simple appliance and a complex data center. If you make an appliance complicated enough to meet enterprise requirements, is it still an appliance?

I love using thought experiments to test ideas. On a business trip, I noticed a coffee machine in my hotel room, and I started asking myself questions. What if I were Mr. Hilton, and I had hundreds of hotels, each with hundreds of rooms, and each room had a Mr. Coffee? What would my problems be—aside from my granddaughter Paris—and how would I solve them?

With so many Mr. Coffees, there will always be some broken ones. How am I going to find them? I could wait for customers to complain, but that would make them unhappy. What if the Mr. Coffee could detect when it's broken? Maybe it could send a signal to alert the maintenance people. That's a good start, but I've got a hotel to run, so I don't really want to be in the Mr. Coffee maintenance business. It'd be best if the Mr. Coffee Company would offer me a service where they detect the signal and they fix the broken machine.

If you look at the coffee maker itself, this updated Mr. Coffee is obviously much more complex than the original. From Mr. Hilton's perspective, however, the new Mr. Coffee is simpler. It is still an appliance, but it's an appliance optimized for the enterprise instead of the home.

In some cases, enterprise customers don't just want you to fix what breaks, but to design, install, and manage the whole solution for them. This was the opposite of our early technical customers who loved learning about the capabilities of a new product. If a feature was interesting enough to catch their attention, then they would experiment until they figured out what it was good for. Better yet, they would often install it themselves, manage it, and even fix it if need be. As a start-up, it was easiest to deal with technical customers. But for success in the broad market, we had to provide a broad range of services. For many years, our professional services organization, which provided these services, was the fastest-growing part of our business.

I thought up the *circle of simplicity* to help us think more deeply about appliances. The idea is that you simplify whatever is inside the circle.

Our very first storage system was so "simple" that there was no good way to make backups (copies of the data in case something bad happens to the original). It was hard to manage because it didn't support the standard tools that people use to control network devices. We made the box itself as simple as possible, but ironically, that made things more complex for the system administrator who managed the box. To simplify life for the sysadmin, we needed to make our product more complex. In other words, we initially drew our circle of simplicity around the box itself, but we should have included the sysadmin inside the circle as well.

Here is the point: Simplicity is not simple.

Oliver Wendell Holmes once said, "I wouldn't give a fig for the simplicity on this side of complexity; I would give my right arm for the simplicity on the far side of complexity." I think that his *far side of complexity* is when you draw the circle of simplicity around everything that matters. Draw too small a circle and your simplicity is naive.

We expanded the circle, made our appliance more complex, and made our customers happier.

We expanded the circle again when customers asked us to store data for Microsoft Windows. (Our first boxes supported only the UNIX operating system.) We briefly considered building a second appliance just for Windows. That would have been easier for us to implement, and probably easier for system administrators to understand. On the other hand, many of our customers told us they were planning to migrate from UNIX to Windows. They needed a storage system that would let users access their files before, during, and after the migration. UNIX and Windows have fundamentally different models of file access, so creating a single system that would let them share data seamlessly was extremely difficult for us—but it sure did simplify life for our customers. They loved it.

To satisfy large enterprise customers you must draw a very large circle of simplicity. They have dozens of data centers scattered across multiple continents, and they have hardware and software from many different vendors. This is the environment they are trying to simplify. Such environments are so complex that simplicity is unachievable. On the other hand, I believe that we can make them simpler than they are. Not simple, but simpler. That is our goal.

••

Enterprise customers demand that their vendors work together. At first I didn't understand. Engineers look at what *should* work, and they often think in terms of industry standards. For instance, an engineer might say, "The NetApp storage speaks NFS over TCP/IP, two standard protocols, and Oracle lives on top of Sun Solaris, which handles those protocols, so that should work fine. And SAP lives on Oracle, which lives on Sun, which handles NFS, which talks to the storage. What could go wrong?" (Don't worry—you aren't expected to understand that. When I said it to customers, most of them didn't either.)

Businesspeople think differently. They know that eventually something will break, and when it does, they worry that a bigger vendor will point at a smaller vendor and say, "That configuration isn't certified. Call us back after you've replaced the storage from that company we've never heard of." At that point, it doesn't matter at all what should work. That's why they insist that all the vendors involved in a solution shake hands and promise, "If something goes wrong, we will fix it together." At first, this insistence on partnerships and certifications frustrated me, especially since we didn't have them. In hindsight, they were right and I was wrong. Eventually things always do break, and it takes cooperating vendors to fix them.

Our experience with Oracle shows how these partnerships can evolve. When customers first started using NAS storage with Oracle databases, in the mid-nineties, both NetApp and Oracle recommended against it. Back then, even I didn't think it made sense to run high-end applications like that over a network. The customers who did it were so happy, however, that we approached Oracle to ask if they would support it. Oracle resisted for years, but—ironically—their engineering department started using NetApp internally. The external message was that *Oracle won't work with NAS*, but the reality was that the programmers developing Oracle's software used NetApp NAS every day. I chatted recently with the CTO of VMware, a company much younger than NetApp, and he sees the same pattern: many software vendors publicly state that their application doesn't work with VMware, even though their programmers use it all the time.

Eventually, Oracle marketing gave in and asked us to sponsor a cost-of-ownership study against our large competitor EMC. They told us which research firm to use and told us to pay for the study. (When the large vendor in a potential partnership asks the small vendor to jump, the correct answer is, "How high, Sir!") The study found that NetApp NAS cost only a quarter as much to buy and operate as SAN storage from EMC, and that was the beginning of a beautiful relationship. Here's how Oracle viewed the world: every customer has a certain amount of money to spend on information technology—some on Oracle and the rest on everything else. If Oracle could help customers save money on "everything else," then hopefully they'd spend more with Oracle. Of course, it was after the dot-com crash that saving money really became important.

A few years ago, Oracle built a data center—one of the largest in the world—to run Oracle applications for their customers, and they chose NetApp NAS for all the storage. Our journey with Oracle symbolizes our entire history with enterprise customers. They went from not trusting us at all to using us internally, and from there to depending on us to provide critical services for their customers.

INTERLUDE
Shark Island—A Parable of Risk and Mass Media

You live on Shark Island, a remote tropical paradise. Your village has a hundred people, and the island has ten such villages—a thousand people in all. The island's name has always seemed a bit odd to you, because you've never seen a shark. In fact, nobody in your village ever has; your grandparents and great-grandparents never even met anybody who saw one. The name came from a story that a hundred years ago, in a village on the far side of the island, a shark once ate a swimmer.

Here's the question. It's a hot, humid day, and a dip in the cool ocean water sure would be refreshing. Do you take a swim, or does that shark attack in a faraway village in a faraway time scare you off?

I've asked many people, and almost always they say, "That doesn't sound dangerous. I think I'll take a swim."

Here's how Shark Island plays out with modern mass media. Shark Island had a thousand people, and one person died in a hundred years. That's an annual death rate of one per hundred thousand. Greater Los Angeles has a population of about 13 million, so the exact same death rate in L.A. would be 130 people per year. Based on the media excitement that one shark attack generates, I'm sure that 130 deaths on L.A. beaches would have people fleeing the seaside all across America.

The problem is, people are wired to act and react like they live on Shark Island—small groups of small villages—rather than in Los Angeles. So media reports spanning millions of people baffle our risk intuition. A death rate that seemed safe in our evolutionary environment creates mass hysteria in our modern environment. No wonder watching television news causes fear in children. What's worse, problems that are much riskier than sharks don't make the headlines because they aren't "newsworthy"—not sexy, violent, or visually appealing. Auto accidents kill forty thousand Americans per year. But sharks get higher ratings.

This started as a rant against mass media and bad risk assessment, but there is also something to learn: Don't plan your risk reduction strategy after reading the newspaper. It's like going to the grocery store when you are hungry. In both cases, you will make bad decisions. The most important risks are rarely in the headlines. In fact, most headlines are about things that are *not* big risks: being unusual is precisely what makes them newsworthy. Children die in car wrecks every day because their parents didn't strap them in, but since it happens so often, it's not news. Perverted strangers almost never kidnap children—it's a risk so low that it's barely worth a second thought—and as a result it's a sensational headline. The business equivalent is that backups fail every day, but data loss from tornados and hurricanes is what makes the front page.

Two lessons, one for business and one for personal life: Verify daily backups before you protect against rare disasters. Check the seatbelt before checking for perverts.

8

STRATEGIC CHANGE

On Reversing Course, Chocolate, Debates, and Core Beliefs

Suppose your church believes, "Jesus Christ is the one true Lord," and then one day you are told, "But Allah is also great. Worship Allah too." That is how I felt when some heretics suggested that NetApp should consider selling SAN in addition to NAS. What's more, James Lau was one of the heretics! It may seem odd that I could have such strong beliefs about a nit-picky technical issue, but I did, and so did many others. In the end, there were even NetApp employees who quit over this dispute, so I think the religious metaphor is appropriate, although—as far as I know—we had no stonings, crucifixions, or jihads. This chapter describes the challenge of confronting radical change in your business strategy.

NAS stands for Network-Attached Storage, while SAN stands for Storage Area Network. From the names alone you can tell they are pretty similar—both about storage and both about networks. It was the classic high-end/low-end situation.

Initially SAN was better for high-end customers, but also much more expensive. NAS was cheaper, improving fast, and had other advantages besides.

In retrospect, I have to admit that there were early hints that we should sell SAN storage. Several market analysts had suggested it. Of course, the same analysts kept telling us that NAS growth would stop, even as we doubled year after year, so I had reason to be skeptical.

Another hint came from a customer, Jason, who was a committed NAS supporter. He loved NAS and used it for all his storage, even when application vendors recommended

---

BFD

Engineers love acronyms and I am no exception. NAS, SAN, NFS, RAID, TCP/IP, NVRAM are common vocabulary at NetApp. Conveying more information with fewer words feels faster and more efficient, but sometimes it can backfire.

One afternoon at Deep Springs, riding with the ranch manager, I mentioned that people were doing amazing things with AI these days. He took immediate interest and said, "Oh, yeah, it's really improved the quality of cattle." Technology eventually reaches all aspects of life, but I had no idea that artificial intelligence had already filtered down to ranching.

"Improved the quality of cattle? I was thinking about the ways it's affecting research in universities and advanced chess strategy," I said.

"Chess strategy?" he asked. "Wait a minute. How in the world can AI have anything to do with playing chess?"

We went back and forth like this for a while, until it finally dawned on me that I was talking about artificial intelligence, but in the ranching world, AI means artificial insemination. Sometimes acronyms waste more time than they save.

SAN. But at one of our customer councils, he came to me and said, "Dave, I wish that you guys would support SAN."

I was stunned. "Jason, you're a NAS guy. Why would you want SAN?"

He said, "Here's the deal. I've got this one application—it's not even that important, but I have to support it—and I ran into some performance problems. I went to the vendor, but they said, 'We don't support NAS, so we won't help until you switch.'" Jason added, "I don't even think the problem is related to NAS. They were looking for an excuse to put me off. So anyway, I went to the purchasing department and told them I needed a small SAN, but they told me they want to reduce the number of vendors. That's where it got ugly. They said, 'Isn't NetApp your storage company? If they can't give you both SAN and NAS, then find a vendor who can.'"

Jason concluded, "It'd sure make my life easier if you would do SAN."

••

The hints were there, but I didn't want to hear them. It wasn't just that I intellectually believed that NAS was better—cheaper and good enough—I was emotionally invested as well. NetApp created the NAS market, it had fueled our success, and we were the primary defender and proponent. On a more personal level, I was the public face of NAS for many years. At storage conferences, our competitors would promote SAN, but I'd be on stage explaining why NAS was better. I would talk about low-end technology moving upmarket, how SAN was doomed for sure, and hadn't they seen this story before with mainframe computers? It is hard to reverse course when you've argued a point of view so many times in public.

Nevertheless, James argued that we should support SAN. James has a habit of being right but is often quiet about his views: he'll state them once, to see if anyone listens, and then keep quiet if they don't. Sometimes I've joked that my job is Spokesman for James, because he comes up with great ideas and says them once, and then I repeat them over and over until people pay attention. I've learned that disagreements with James often occur because one of us knows something that the other does not. Usually it's not something obvious; it's a hidden assumption. Sometimes you have to keep digging—keep arguing, but I mean that in a friendly, searching-for-the-truth kind of way—to figure out what the hidden assumption is, because once you expose it, then the right answer suddenly comes into clear focus. Given this experience, I was comfortable disagreeing with James, fully expecting that we'd eventually work it out. In this case, the discussion went on for many months. (This willingness to cooperatively disagree, working together to try and get to the right solution, is an aspect of our culture that I try to promote.)

My argument was that the NAS market was growing fast enough. Many of our employees joined NetApp because they believed in NAS. We represented the new, not the old. Our sales staff depended on *SAN is Bad* to sell. Also, the marketplace for SAN was big and crowded. We would be coming in as the newest and smallest producer—never a good place to be—and we would be playing catch-up for a long time. The resources invested in SAN would be better spent improving NAS. Why risk our edge and our culture to do something we knew was inferior?

The flaw with my arguments, James said, was that they had a NetApp bias because they were based on our employees, engineers, and salespeople. James looked at our market opportunity and our potential customers. He argued that SAN was an enormous market—much larger than NAS—and many companies wouldn't even consider doing business with us because they thought NAS was too low-end. If we could do SAN, then at least we'd be in the door. And finally, he argued that much of the engineering investment required for SAN would be needed anyway for NAS. As we moved upmarket, our customers requested that we add more and more high-end SAN features into our NAS system. Adding support for SAN's special network wasn't that big a deal—he argued—compared to all the other work we had to do anyway.

Back and forth it went.

Dan, our CEO, wanted to get the Board of Directors up to speed on SAN and NAS, so he asked James and me to share our views. Most CEOs try to hide internal dissent from their boards, not display it front and center, so it is a testament to Dan's open and honest relationship with our board that he would encourage two founders to debate in front of them.

I remember Don Valentine, the chairman of the board, asking me, "Have any of your customers ever asked you for SAN?"

"Yes," I admitted.

This was shortly after the dot-com crash, and Valentine's input was simple: "In this economy, if someone wants to give you their money, I recommend that you take it." This clarity of thought is why Valentine gets to be chairman.

James was right and I was wrong.

••

Now my challenge was to explain this about-face to our employees. How could we overcome the religious zealotry that I described earlier? As VP of engineering, I had learned that sometimes the best way to defend a decision is to point out its flaws.

Let's say you have decided to pursue Plan A. As a manager, it is part of your job to defend and explain that decision to folks who work for you. So when someone marches into your office to explain that Plan A sucks, and that Plan Z would be much better, what do you do?

My old instinct was to listen to Plan Z, say what I didn't like about it, and to describe as best as I could why Plan A was better. Of course, the person has already seen these same arguments in the e-mail I sent announcing the decision, but since they didn't agree, they must not have heard me clearly, so I'd better repeat my argument again, right? I can report that this seldom worked very well.

It works much better if I start out by agreeing: "Yep. Plan Z is a reasonable plan. Not only for the reasons you mentioned, but here are two more advantages. And Plan A—the plan that we chose—not only has the flaws that you mentioned, but here are three more flaws." The effect of this technique is amazing. It seems completely counterintuitive, but even if you don't convince people that your plan is better, hearing you explain your plan's flaws—and their plan's advantages—makes them much more comfortable.

Here's what I think is going on. When upper management sends down a decision, it can be scary, because people wonder whether they understand the consequences. If you show that you do understand the pitfalls of your plan, it reassures people that you didn't decide blindly. If you knew all those problems and still chose Plan A, perhaps it's not as bad as they thought. Ideally, being open about pros and cons leads to a conversation in

The Pig

I once overheard James talking about me on his cell phone. He said, "Arguing with Dave is like mud wrestling with a pig. Eventually you realize the pig likes it."

which you can convince them that Plan A really is best. But whether that happens or not, they'll definitely leave feeling better than if you simply pretended that your plan was perfect and the alternative stupid. (Of course, if the person raises flaws or alternatives that you hadn't considered, then you may need to reopen the decision.)

This is part of a larger philosophy. I want an environment where it's okay to openly discuss the pros and cons of ideas and plans. Every idea has advantages and disadvantages. I shouldn't take it as a personal attack when someone points out a flaw. When you choose a plan, you choose it warts and all. The best way to succeed is to be open about the flaws and work to address them.

It helps to avoid a strong link between ideas and people. If I think of an idea as mine, then when you insult it, you are insulting me. If I think of an idea as a hypothesis that we can investigate together and maybe modify together, then we can discuss flaws and alternatives without making it personal. When ideas are a joint project with multiple people contributing, you end up with something better than any one person could think up alone.

In keeping with this style of thinking, Andy Watson—one of our technical spokesmen—suggested that we have a public debate about NAS and SAN, open to the entire company. "But the decision has already been made," I said.

"It doesn't matter," Andy replied, "What matters is that everyone in the company hears all of the issues that we considered in making this decision."

We had the debate, and even though everyone knew that the outcome was predetermined, the debaters didn't hold back. Four anti-SAN people made their best cases against (the exact same arguments that they had used before we made the decision), and four pro-SAN people made the case in favor. I had been anti-SAN, but I decided not to argue that side, because the symbolism of a co-founder arguing against the decision in public would be too strong. Instead, I was the moderator.

I don't know whether the public debate actually changed anybody's mind, but many people told me that it made them much more comfortable with the decision. Allowing the anti-SAN people to make their strongest case in public made it clear that we had made the decision with our eyes wide open. It is tempting, after a decision like this, to whitewash the debate and pretend that everyone agreed all along. Our approach worked better in the long run.

••

Companies periodically face the question of whether to expand their market focus. If your current market is large enough or growing fast enough, then you may have no need to broaden. This was my argument with respect to NAS: it was growing fast and I expected that to continue. However, there is a second reason to broaden your horizon, which is that your market is on a collision course with another—two markets used to be separate, but now they are converging into one larger market.

We had faced the issue of colliding markets years earlier with UNIX and Windows. We started doing storage for UNIX computers, and that market seemed large enough, but many of our customers asked us to support Windows as well. At first we resisted, telling them that the UNIX market was plenty large for our growth. We might do Windows eventually, but it wasn't a priority.

Then our customers explained more clearly. This was in the mid-nineties, when many CIOs were hoping to convert most—some said all—of their computers from UNIX to Windows. One customer put it like this: "As we do this conversion, we need a place to store our data that can be accessed by Windows as well as UNIX. We can't convert all at once, but we still need to access all of our data." The UNIX and Windows storage markets were coming together, and when we developed a system that supported both, it gave us a strong strategic advantage that helped support our repeated doublings in the late nineties.

A similar convergence was happening between SAN and NAS. If you strip away the technical details, SAN and NAS are like flavors of ice cream. Some people love chocolate; others prefer vanilla. If you run an ice cream shop, you'd best sell both. I can imagine Jason as a chocolate lover, explaining to the owners of a chocolate-only ice cream shop why they should also sell vanilla: "You know I love chocolate, but my wife wants vanilla, and she won't come here with me unless you have vanilla for her. I don't even like vanilla, but I wish you would sell it."

In the early nineties, NAS was a separate, low-end market, because the networks that it ran on were so slow and unreliable. As I described in Chapter Four, the dot-com boom drove improvements in both networking and NAS. People started solving the same problems with NAS that they had previously solved with SAN, and the two markets started to become one.

Changing a core belief is hard and full of risk. The payoff, however, was worth it. Since we made this decision, NetApp has quadrupled in size. It's hard to second-guess success like that. As my emotional attachment to NAS has faded, I can acknowledge that SAN sometimes has clear technical advantages over NAS. Also, change is expensive: you may need to retrain people, or you may need to replace old equipment that still meets your needs. Even when NAS is theoretically better, it may not be worth switching. I have come to believe that money has momentum: a multibillion-dollar market like SAN will not disappear anytime soon.

On the other hand, NAS and Ethernet have continued to improve over the years. Technology improves faster than customer requirements, and the arguments in favor of NAS are stronger than ever. In order to gain credibility in the SAN market, NetApp became completely neutral—supporting both technologies equally—but now that we are recognized as one of the top SAN vendors, neck-and-neck with EMC, we are starting to promote NAS more heavily again. Some of the world's largest companies use NAS for mission-critical applications in some of the world's largest data centers, and they have saved enormous amounts of money as a result. We have any flavor you want, but if you are undecided, we recommend that you try the chocolate.

INTERLUDE
Speckled-Egg Thinking

An article about cliff-dwelling seagulls and the challenges they face helped shape my view of human nature. Small rocks are always falling down the cliffs and landing in the birds' nests. That's bad, because rocks can crack eggs and hurt chicks, so the gulls push them out of their nests. Sometimes eggs roll out of the nest and onto the rock ledge. The birds naturally pull escaped eggs back into their nests.

How do the gulls decide what to push out and what to pull in? Or to put it another way, how do bird brains identify stones and eggs? To find out, researchers put objects with various shapes and colors into the nests. The gulls pushed out anything with sharp, pointy corners. They apparently identify rocks by feel, ignoring color. Next the researchers put the same objects outside the nest to see how birds identified eggs. This time, the gulls ignored shape. They simply pulled in anything with the same brown and speckled color as their eggs.

To the scientific mind, this raised an obvious question: How would the birds respond to a brown and speckled cube? It's pointy like a rock, but colored like an egg. Put this evil egg into a nest, and here's what happens. First, the bird pushes it out, because of the sharp corners. Then the bird pulls it back into the nest, because of the color. Out of the nest and into the nest, all day long. Each individual act makes sense, but repeating to exhaustion does not. The birds can't step back and see the big picture.

You might conclude that seagulls are stupid, which is true, but it misses the point. In their natural environment, with no sadistic ornithologists, the gulls' simple rules work perfectly: sharp equals-stone and speckled-equals-egg. Remember, birds fly, so the lighter their brains the better. Why carry extra baggage? Absent meddling scientists, these simple rules may be the best possible design.

What does this have to do with business or human behavior?

People also have instinctive behaviors, but unlike gulls, we no longer live in our natural environment. During most of our evolutionary history, humans lived in small nomadic bands with just a few dozen members; the most advanced technology was hide tents and flint arrowheads. No wonder we see so much speckled-egg behavior—behavior that seems meaningless and futile—in modern corporations that equip employees with BlackBerrys and Web browsers and pack thousands of them into small cubicles.

People get frustrated with the limitations of humans in a way that they don't with physical objects. Someone who is building a bridge will ask: How wide is the river? What materials can I build with, and how heavy or strong are they? Bridge builders don't complain that the river should be narrower or that cotton candy should have more tensile strength so they could build with that. They deal with the physical reality.

But with people, we often expect perfection. We get angry that people aren't more rational, or more persistent, or more empathetic, or—whatever. If you are building a company, you have to deal with how people actually are. People are not perfect little cogs that you can bolt into place. Our human brains are absolutely amazing—full of insight and magic—and yet also deeply flawed, because they were designed for a different world from the one we live in today.

Good leaders must spot speckled-egg thinking and help people step back to see the big picture.

9

VISION

On Whining, Eras, Future History, and the Meaning of Life

By 2003, I was happy, hopeful, and oddly confused. We had pretty much recovered from the dot-com crash. We were growing again, and our profit levels were healthy. I should have been pleased, but instead I was anxious. What we were doing was obviously working, given how well we'd bounced back, but I didn't understand where we were headed. In the hypergrowth period, our goal was always simple: double last year's revenues. That worked great, all the way up to a billion dollars. After the crash, our goal was simple again: return to health. But when we reached a billion the second time, it wasn't clear what our next big milestone should be.

Two questions kept me up at night: Where should we go next? and How will we get there? Doubling annually was not a realistic option, both because of our size and because the economy was still slow. I fell back on an old management technique: I began to whine.

After becoming VP of engineering, I noticed that when I whined about things, people would run off and try to fix them. (It's great being the boss.) At first my lesson was that I'd better complain as accurately as possible. The better I could describe what I didn't like, the more likely my staff was to fix the right problem. Finally I had an epiphany: Whining is the evil twin to vision. Accurate whining is a careful description of how you wish the world was not. Vision is a careful description of how you wish the world would become. Whining is a sign that you have an opportunity for vision. They may be closely related, but vision is much more motivational.

Applying that lesson, I arranged a series of interviews to ask Dan's staff and others what they thought we could hope to achieve, given our market share and competitive position. What did we *need* to achieve?

Writing helps me clarify my thinking and make decisions, both professional and personal, so I took the notes from my interviews and turned them into a short paper. On a lark, I

The Brown-Nose Rule

At NetApp there's a well-known saying: *What interests my boss fascinates me.* On the one hand, it is a silly little observation. On the other hand, it suggests a possible management technique. If you express interest in an area, it is likely that folks further down in the organization will become interested or even fascinated. Why not make a point of identifying issues that you think deserve more attention and expressing interest in them? Employees will likely focus on what you care about.

There is, of course, a potential downside. Especially at the topmost levels, leaders have to be careful what they express interest in. I heard a story about film mogul George Lucas. Walking around Skywalker started writing in the past tense, as if our hopes had already come to pass and I was describing how it all happened. (The inspiration came from a science fiction series by Robert Heinlein called the Future History Stories.) I shared my Future History with the people I had interviewed, to see if I got their input right. Some sent me long e-mails clarifying their thoughts, and some even wrote in the past tense—future history style—so that I could incorporate their words directly into my paper. It became a group effort.

This Future History took on a life of its own. The VP of marketing at the time, Mark Santora, asked me if his staff could read it, and when I agreed, he asked if I would lead a strategy offsite for his group, using the paper as a foundation. (Remember, I was still VP of engineering at this point, so writing corporate strategy documents and leading offsite meetings for other groups was not my day job.)

That offsite was so well received that Dan asked me to do the same thing for his staff. The two offsites provided feedback

Ranch during construction, he noticed a newly painted building and mentioned to an aide—just in passing—that he'd thought it was going to be a slightly darker shade of brown. The next day, George walked by and saw that the building was now painted a darker brown. He told his aide, "I was just making a comment—I didn't mean you should repaint it!" George walked by the building the next day, and it was light brown again. I do not know if these events actually happened, but they ring true.

I was in a meeting where a VP joked about something that Dan "found very interesting." A member of the VP's staff responded, "What interests my boss's boss really clenches up my anus."

to refine the history's three key conclusions. The first conclusion was that we must grow in order to survive. Even at a billion dollars in revenue, we were small and vulnerable compared with competitors like EMC, HP, and IBM. Second, we must learn how to become a long-term strategic supplier to large companies for their enterprise data center requirements. After the dot-com collapse, that's where the money was. And third, we must target the SAN market because that's what many enterprise customers wanted. Through the group effort of developing the Future History, Dan's staff agreed that these were our most critical goals; looking back, we were right. It's no coincidence that Chapters Seven and Eight of this book were on enterprise customers and SAN—goals two and three.

Next we used the Future History as a foundation for our annual Senior Leader's Meeting, an offsite with our top hundred people, and finally we decided to send the paper to every employee in the company. The decision to share it so openly was controversial. Some felt that the risk of competitors getting a copy was too great. Dan and I concluded that—while there was some risk—there was an even greater risk in trying to execute a strategy without telling our own employees what it was. It is astounding how many companies do attempt that. Trust is a two-way street. If the management team, as part of our culture, wants the employees to trust us, then we ought to trust them.

I don't know how to measure the effect of the Future History. On the one hand, you could argue that it was simply a normal business planning process cloaked in a science fiction device. On the other hand, I think it caught people's imagination in a way that a normal—dull—business plan would not. Many groups in the company have since written their own future histories, focusing on their own part of the business. We even developed a simulation or "business game," like Monopoly on steroids, based on the Future History, to help teach managers what we are trying to accomplish.

••

In the interviews, I learned to get people into a "future history mood" by talking about the past. It is hard to get people to think more than a year in the future, but looking back many years prepares you to look forward many years. Don't just extrapolate today's concerns; try to spot emerging trends that could trigger a new era. By definition, an era is marked by such radical change that success requires new strategies: if the issues aren't radically different, then it isn't a new era.

I divide NetApp's history into four eras: start-up, hypergrowth, crash-and-recover, and enterprise-customer. In our start-up era, we invented and developed a product, raised money, found customers, hired a new CEO, became profitable, and went public. The big issue was to define NetApp: what our products should be, which customers to go after, and how to reach them. In the hypergrowth era that followed, after the IPO, we understood our products and customers, and the big challenge was to drive fast growth without breaking our company or our culture.

The transition from one era to another can be difficult to spot because most eras have roots that go deep into earlier ones. We had issues with fast growth even in the start-up era, but they weren't so dangerous until we got larger. The roots of the enterprise-customer era went all the way back to our Love Yahoo/Love Cisco program, but it was years before we recognized the enormous change required to satisfy traditional enterprise customers. What matters isn't the exact day of transition but the recognition that a new set of strategic issues is emerging.

I don't know if it's possible to reliably predict the details of future eras. Probably not. Second best, and still quite useful, is to notice early that a new one is beginning. Sometimes it is obvious. There was no mistaking the end of hypergrowth and the beginning of crash-and-recover. But other times, the first hint may be a feeling of confusing discomfort about your old strategy. Has a new era started? Are old assumptions still true (SAN is evil), or is it time to take a fundamentally different path (SAN is redeemed)? Living in the past can be deadly.

When you plan a quarter or a year ahead, it is easy to stick to incremental change, limited by what seems easy. When you spot a new era, it can drive much larger change because you look forward several years and ask what it will take to be successful or even to avoid being killed in the new era. You get more creative when you realize that you must do much more than you thought possible. Remember, I believe in magic.

Writing historically about the future requires you to give the detailed story about how you got to your desired spot—not just state an audacious goal. In the end, is a future history really any different from a normal business plan? Maybe it's like follow-through after you hit a baseball or a golf ball. It doesn't really matter what you do after the ball leaves the club, but your state of mind creates subtle mechanics earlier in the swing that do make a difference.

••

At Deep Springs College, I learned how satisfying it can feel when your work links directly to people's basic needs. I spent two summers with a fellow cowboy minding the school's herd of cattle in the mountains, a day's ride from the nearest town. (You may insert your own Brokeback joke here.) We had two small shacks and a side of beef that we slaughtered ourselves. A side of beef will keep all summer if you expose it to the cold at night and wrap it up in a sleeping bag under your bed during the day. We had no running water, just a spring that fed into a horse trough.

The experience taught me a lot about what you do and don't need to live happily. Life was great despite the rough surroundings. Two previous summers I had worked as a programmer, and the contrast made me realize how distant most people's jobs are from anything that matters. Up there on the mountain, I was taking care of food. Meat. It wasn't abstract at all. Perhaps it is the memory of work that is so real that pushes me to find what matters in our work at NetApp. I sometimes wonder if my aspirations for NetApp's culture are an attempt to recreate the sense of community and meaning I felt at Deep Springs.

In most jobs, it is hard for people to figure out their place in the world or what makes their work meaningful, but it's important to try. Remember Maslow's lesson: once people have satisfied their basic needs—food, housing, security for their family—they want to contribute to something greater. People must all figure this out for themselves, but perhaps I can provide an example by sharing my own thinking.

It's easy to understand why meat matters—it satisfies a physical requirement—but to people whose life does not revolve around information technology, my passion for data storage may seem bewildering. Twenty years ago, data was dry and uninteresting, but today it is becoming increasingly important in people's everyday lives. It used to be quarterly financial results for a corporation or the schematics for a clock radio; now it is your address book, family photos, or a movie of your child's first steps. I believe there will be a generation of children who are missing big chunks of their lives because their parents didn't understand about backups. When fleeing a burning building, people used to grab the family photo album; today you ought to grab the PC. It has your correspondence, financial records, even your will—along with your photos. Our data is becoming who we are.

We have entered the Age of Data. This is good for NetApp financially, but it also helps make our work meaningful—in a way that can inspire NetApp employees to care, to come to work with passion. The last thirty years of computer history support my claim of a new age.

The Personal Computing Age: In the 1980s, we put a computer on every desk. At the start of the decade, only an elite (and nerdy) few had computers. The PC was introduced in 1981, the Mac in 1984, and by the end of the decade, they were everywhere. Computer companies like Compaq, Microsoft, Apple, and Sun became major IT players.

The Networking Age: In the 1990s, we networked all those computers together. Early in the decade, the most common method of data transfer was "sneaker net"—walking around with floppy disks. By the end, every business computer was connected to the Internet. This time it was Cisco that rose to the ranks of major IT player.

The Age of Data: Some people think that what matters about the Internet is that everyone is connected. I disagree. I

How to Castrate a Bull

Given the book's title, I couldn't omit this lesson. When castrating a bull, the best thing for all involved is to act when it is still a bull calf. It is safer and easier for both you and the animal. Despite popular misconceptions, castration apparently does not hurt very much—dehorning and branding both cause much more bellowing.

The first step, after immobilizing the bull, is to grab the base of the scrotum tightly, making sure that the testicles are in the sack. They are hard to retrieve if they escape into the body cavity. Now cut off the bottom third of the scrotum, below the testicles. Bovine testicles look like two white cigars, each connected to the body by a long, thin cord. Grab them firmly with a palms-down grip, letting the cords thread through your fingers. Take a dull knife and fray the cords all the way through. Do not use a normal back-and-forth cutting motion, but a side-to-side scraping motion. Warning: Do not use a sharp knife no matter how much the bull begs. A sharp cut bleeds dangerously, but a dull fray creates more surface area to induce clotting. Leave the wound undressed and release the animal. Repeat until you've finished the herd. Then cross *Castrate a Bull* off your list of things to do before you die.

say that what matters is the data that they choose to share over those connections. Companies that focus on the data—like Google for searching it and NetApp for storing and managing it—have become major IT players.

Data is important partly because there is so much of it. Disk drives today are so big that they are hard to fill. Once you could fill a drive by typing. Now you can type for the rest of your life and barely make a dent. With digital voice compression, you can talk for the rest of your life and not fill a disk. We are almost to the point that you can look for the rest of your life (digital photos and movies).

But our customers fill millions of drives a year. Where can so much data come from?

The first source is computers—they generate data much faster than people. To save money, automakers crash-test virtual cars instead of real ones, each collision creating an enormous amount of data. Industrial Light & Magic, which did the computer-generated special effects for *Star Wars* and *Jurassic Park*, can create up to 10 terabytes a day, equivalent to 20 million copies of this book.

The second source is millions of people typing at once. One person typing can't fill a disk, but millions can. Yahoo has a quarter billion e-mail accounts.

The third source is scanning the real world. Look how quickly digital cameras and camcorders consume space. Now imagine the data from a billion-dollar satellite. Oil companies scan the earth; genetic researchers scan the DNA from thousands of people. The amount of information in the physical world staggers the imagination.

And finally, there are multiple copies of all this data, both because people share and because they make backup copies to protect against loss.

••

To get a feeling for why people's data matters to them, I like to ask what problems they face if they lose their data. Earlier I mentioned that for Southwest Airlines, the problems are that they can't sell tickets and all their planes must land immediately.

One of our German customers is a brewery. They are legally required to identify and track every bottle they fill. If they can't access their data for more than ten minutes, then the beer must stop flowing: a real incentive to keep data safe and available.

My favorite answer came in Israel. In Israel it's easy to tell when you are meeting with military people, because they are carrying guns. The ones in blue uniforms carry small side-arms that they keep in their holsters during the meeting. The ones in green uniforms carry machine guns that they lay on the table in front of them. If the greens and blues alternate at the table, the guns all fit fine, but if two greens sit next to each other, one of them has to balance his machine gun precariously against the side of his chair.

I asked a blue-uniformed man, "What bad things happen if you can't access your data?" He looked back at me across the table, his hand resting on his holstered gun, and replied, "People die." It didn't occur to me until later to wonder whether he meant his own people, or whoever sold him the equipment.

Bottom line: No data means no beer and people die.

Data about people has become so pervasive that it will take decades for our legal system to figure it out. You might imagine we could handle digital data with the same laws as paper, but consider this. One disk drive that fits in the palm of your hand can hold the name, address, government ID, and credit card number of everyone on the planet. If you printed all the data on a one-terabyte disk, it would take 20 million pounds of paper. Imagine trying to protect that much paper. You might hire guards, or build a locked warehouse, but you certainly wouldn't worry about somebody sneaking it into their pocket. The legal system hasn't caught up.

To be sure, there are many laws already. Banks must keep financial records for seven years. Digital medical records must be stored for the life of the patient plus seven years. There are also many laws about privacy. But questions of data ownership are still troublesome. Should Amazon own the record of all the books I have ever bought, or should I? I think of my financial records as mine, but my bank and my broker think they own them. Medical records are even more personal. Are they mine or my doctor's?

Professor Deirdre Mulligan from the University of California, Berkeley, argues that ownership is the wrong mental model. I have a strong interest in my own medical records, but my doctor does too: the collection of medical records that he has created over the years documents his career. In a malpractice suit, he may need them to demonstrate his competence. When a medical center comes under scrutiny, the records of all doctors and patients at the center may be required to understand the patterns of care.

It is better to think in terms of rights and responsibilities associated with data, according to Mulligan. As a patient, I have the right to access my medical records, to transfer them to a new doctor, and so on. My doctor and the medical center have rights as well, but also responsibilities. They must keep the records safe and private. There is a fuzzy, blended combination of rights and responsibilities that are shared between my doctor, my medical center, and me.

As we store more private information about people, data management becomes entangled with philosophical issues of ownership, rights, responsibilities, and ethics. None of the technical issues of data management go away, but to really help our customers solve their problems, we also have to focus on managing data rights and responsibilities. Maybe data stewardship is the best term to capture this idea. All of this dramatically broadens the business scope for NetApp. I've always loved working on hard technical problems, but it's especially rewarding that our work also matters at a higher societal level.

••

Writing a future history for NetApp made me question what I wanted in my own life and career. Perhaps everyone should occasionally write down their personal future history, looking for eras in their life and asking whether, perhaps, a new one has begun. So far, my career at NetApp has had several eras—independent of the company eras—and I try to keep my eyes open for emerging trends or that feeling of confusing discomfort that could signal the start of my next one.

In my years as VP of engineering, the Future History project gave me more satisfaction than anything else I had done, and that made me wonder whether I was in the right job. Managing lots of people had never been a goal of mine. Maybe I'd find more satisfaction in a role that let me focus on the big picture for the whole company.

I shared my feelings with Tom Mendoza and asked his advice. He suggested that I go for it. He pointed out that it would be easier to hire a new VP of engineering than to find a new founder for the company-wide strategy work that I'd been doing. So I ended that era of my career and began another.

No traditional corporate title describes my job. *Chief Philosophy Officer* is the best I've come up with, because I ask the timeless philosophical questions: Who are we? Where did we come from? Where are we going? Mostly I want to keep NetApp headed in the right direction and make sure it is a healthy place for people to work. After three or four years, we completed almost all the goals in our first Future History, so I wrote a second one. I recently met Gary Hamel and read his book, *The Future of Management*, about companies that reinvent the way they are run, and that's got me thinking about how NetApp should change. In addition, Dan and Tom are both about ten years older than me, and we need to ensure a smooth transition as they retire and the next generation of leaders takes over. There is plenty of work for a chief philosophy officer.

I am happier without so many people reporting to me. I don't like being the boss of people; I'd rather figure out what ought to happen and then convince people from the side. Here's a personal preference that I can't explain: in a medieval kingdom, I'd rather be the king's trusted and influential adviser than be the king himself. However, I don't regret my time running engineering. Without the experience of managing large budgets and many people, I wouldn't be qualified for my current role in a company our size. That was a valuable era for me.

Perhaps this willingness to keep reevaluating my personal role is what has allowed me to remain at NetApp—contributing positively, I like to think—long after most founders give up or are fired.

Sometimes people ask me, "What does it feel like to have built such a large company?" My response is that I didn't build it. It was more like planting a seed. Suppose you planted an acorn, and then twenty years later you have a large oak tree. How would you feel if someone asked, "What did it feel like to build that tree?" Sure, you planted it, maybe watered it and picked the weeds, but you didn't build it. I think of NetApp the same way. I am proud of what we have accomplished, and I am proud of my role in helping to get it started, and in guiding it over the years, but it seems very odd to think of it as something that I have built. Maybe proud papa is a closer analogy. There is an organic magic in the way companies grow.

If there is a secret to our success, I would say it is the recognition that people crave meaning in their lives, and they want to be part of something that matters. We want work to be something that people love (most days) and think is important. I know we don't always succeed, but this is what Dan, Tom, James, and I all aspire to. Dan told me that, of all NetApp's accomplishments, the one he is most proud of is that we have appeared many years in a row in *Fortune* magazine's list of the "One Hundred Best Companies to Work For."

Some people may have different perspectives on and interpretations of these events. That's okay. This is my version, but like I said, there's more than one way to tell a story. My mother, for instance, doesn't deny advising me against a career in computers, but she says her more important message was that I should find something I love and work hard. Which brings me to my last important business lesson:

Always listen to my mother.

APPENDIX A
Early NetApp Business Plan

This is a very early NetApp business plan, requesting seed-round funding, written by Mike Malcolm, James Lau, and me in the two months following our first discussions. As you can see, we did not yet have NetApp as a company name. Back then we used the term *server*, as opposed to *storage system*, so you'll see some terminology differences from the rest of the book. In the book, I changed our early name from 1-800-SERVERS to 1-800-STORAGE to reduce confusion. Included at the end of the business plan is a preliminary specification for the product itself.

Be careful what lessons you take from this. Given that we never did manage to convince any venture capitalists to fund us until after we shipped product, perhaps budding entrepreneurs would be best off not copying this plan. On the other hand, a first-round investment of $1 million would have yielded over $2 billion worth of stock eight years later, so perhaps the real lesson is for VCs. Looking back, I can see that some areas came out just as we predicted, and in other areas we were completely off base. I'd say the biggest flaw is that the plan focuses too much on markets, technology, and competitors, but not enough on sales strategy or customers, which are equally important. That reflects the strengths and weaknesses of the three of us as the founding team of a company.

1-800-SERVERS
Business Plan Overview
January 16, 1992

This confidential working document outlines the business plan for a proposed new company.

Mission
Develop, manufacture, distribute and support a family of file servers. Establish and maintain the market position of best price/performance.

Background
The rapid evolution and deployment of distributed computing technology has created enormous demands on the performance, capacity, and reliability of data storage servers. By the end of this decade, hundreds of millions of personal computers and workstations will require millions of servers. The servers, as well as the personal computers and workstations, will become commodity products.

Servers will primarily fall into two categories: file servers and database servers. Database servers will become increasingly important as client-server computing is used for more business applications. However, file servers will continue to be the most common repository of data in distributed computing networks.

Most personal computers use proprietary file server protocols, the most common of which is Novell's NetWare. Almost all workstations use the open file server protocol, NFS. Today there are approximately 2.2 million workstations and personal computers that use NFS. The NFS market is much smaller than the NetWare market; it is also more open and less competitive.

More than a third of a million new workstations were shipped in 1990. Roughly one NFS file server is required for every seven workstations. Thus, approximately 50,000 NFS file servers were sold in 1990, representing over one billion dollars in sales. At current growth rates, sales should exceed $2 billion this year.

In the past four years, a small number of startups have produced NFS file servers. The most successful of these are Auspex and Epoch.

Auspex produces NFS servers with very high throughput performance. An Auspex server can handle up to eight heavily loaded Ethernets. Epoch's product has much lower performance, but it provides an additional layer in the memory hierarchy: optical disk. The Epoch NFS file server is aimed at users who require huge amounts of storage. Both Auspex and Epoch are pursuing relatively narrow niches in the NFS market.

The Vision

There is an excellent opportunity to create a new company to provide commodity-like file servers that can be purchased at the departmental level, installed as easily as household appliances, and managed by users with no training or experience.

The company would initially develop an NFS file server that is differentiated by the following four features:

1. *High Availability:* It will run for longer periods of time between outages. Restart times will be very short. A fault-tolerant disk array and uninterruptible power supply will provide high data integrity.

2. *Easy Administration:* Installation will be trivial with no configuration decisions to make or parameters to set. All implementation details will be hidden. Little documentation and no training will be required.

3. *High Performance:* Lowest latency and full bandwidth utilization with one or two Ethernets.

4. *Low Price:* Under $10,000 entry price. Price/performance will be from five to ten times better than today's NFS servers.

The key idea is to design the product from the ground up to be a file server and nothing but a file server. While the product will use open protocols, it will not be programmable by customers or by independent software vendors. It will not run any application programs.

The product will *not* run UNIX. Avoiding the complexities of UNIX will enable the product to achieve high performance and easy system management. (All existing NFS file servers are based on UNIX, or something slower and more complicated to manage—such as MVS. Auspex products are unique in that the NFS network requests do not go through the UNIX processor; this appears to be a major contributor to their high performance.)

The distribution strategy will exploit the product's ease of installation. In North America, a strategy similar to the "Dell Model" will be used to make it as easy for customers to order and install an NFS file server as it is to order an external disk drive from La Cie and install it on a Macintosh.

Follow-on products could include a lower entry price model, a higher-performance model using a copper FDDI interface, and automatic file backup capabilities.

The software and hardware would be designed to facilitate the future development of non-NFS file servers. For example, a NetWare file server could be developed using the same philosophy, the same hardware, and most of the same software. Eventually it may also be possible to apply a similar approach to database servers, through a strategic alliance with a major database vendor.

The Proposed LADDIS Benchmark

Until recently, there was no consistent way to measure or compare the performance of NFS servers. The LADDIS Group has proposed an NFS server benchmark that will enable users to easily compare the performance of NFS servers. The LADDIS benchmark will encourage customers to view NFS servers as commodity products, and help to undermine their current brand loyalties.

The acronym LADDIS was derived from the names of the participating NFS vendors: Legato, Auspex, Data General, DEC, Interphase and Sun. The LADDIS Group submitted the proposed benchmark to SPEC (Systems Performance Evaluation Cooperative) in August 1991. As with other proposed SPEC benchmarks, the LADDIS benchmark must be scrutinized by all SPEC member companies before adoption.

The LADDIS benchmark generates a synthetic load of client requests that comprises a realistic mix of operations—read, write, lookup, etc.—and measures the response times of the server. The result is a graph of average response time (in milliseconds) as a function of throughput (in NFS operations per second).

Evaluation copies of PRE_LADDIS Version 0.0.11 will be available in February 1992. The official benchmark should be released by SPEC in late 1992. It is written in C and runs on most UNIX workstations.

The proposed LADDIS benchmark is already receiving attention in the UNIX trade press. Published LADDIS results will be a key tool for selling our proposed NFS server products.

The Product Plan

The software will be based on a real-time kernel. Some components will be derived from public domain software, such as the file system, the TCP/UDP/IP stack, and NFS. Proprietary components and modifications will be developed to achieve extremely simple system administration, high reliability, fast system restart, low response times for NFS operations, and high throughput performance.

The first product will use commodity board components based on EISA bus, an Intel 386 or 486 processor, an uninterruptible power supply, an array of disk drives (either 3.5-inch or 2.5-inch), an optical tape drive for backup, and one or two Ethernet interfaces. Storage capacity will be expandable from one to 20 gigabytes. It will be possible to insert new disk drives without disrupting client workstations. The goal will be to ship products within the first year to 18 months of operation.

The second product will integrate the network and disk interfaces onto the processor board, using a novel architecture to reduce manufacturing costs and to provide significant performance improvements.

Product development strategy will be guided by the following (somewhat inconsistent goals):

- Focus on developing unique added value.

- Focus on software; minimize hardware development and in-house manufacturing. Use partners to obtain hardware without losing the flexibility to change partners or do our own hardware in the future.

- Minimize royalty payments to third parties.

Competition

Sun Microsystems is the main supplier of NFS file servers. Sun sells over 2/3 of all NFS file servers. Our initial product will be positioned to cost significantly less than Sun's lower-end server, with performance comparable to their high-end servers.

It is unlikely that Sun will be able to produce a server that performs as well, or costs as little, for several reasons:

- Sun's server hardware is inherently more expensive because it has lower production volumes than our components, and it must be capable of supporting Solaris (UNIX System V Release 4)—which requires GUI hardware, a CD player, and one or more powerful RISC processors to achieve performance.

- Sun is unlikely to produce a file server that does not use UNIX.

- Sun's move to UNIX System V Release 4 will probably introduce significant new performance problems that will take years to correct.

- The culture among software engineers at Sun places little value on performance.

- The structure of Sun—with SunSoft doing NFS and UNIX, and SMCC doing hardware—makes it difficult for Sun to produce products that provide creative software-hardware system solutions.

- Sun's distribution costs will likely remain high due to the level of technical support required to install and manage a Sun server.

- Sun is focused on desktop workstations because desktop products have higher volumes than servers.

Sun will still be a formidable competitor through their installed base, channel control and FUD. Sun could react to losing sales by launching a performance improvement project and providing deep discounts. Hopefully, by being too far behind the power curve, Sun would eventually concede the file server market and focus on workstations. (Our product could help increase the size of Sun's workstation market by decreasing the customer's total capital investment and cost of ownership.)

No other workstation vendor appears to have an NFS server strategy that is more viable than that of Sun. Many workstation vendors do not provide file servers at all.

Auspex will not be able to compete at the low end of the NFS server market with their current architecture. Their product requires multiple processors, a VME bus, and UNIX. The Auspex architecture is inherently harder to manage and more expensive than that of the proposed product. We also expected our product to have significantly faster response times (lower latency) than can be achieved using the Auspex architecture.

Distribution

The goal would be to achieve a high market share as quickly as possible so that competitors have little time to react.

In North America, a small highly-focused direct sales force will call on large and strategic accounts. Eventually, most orders will be taken by phone using an 800 number. All servers will be sold with a 30-day return policy, and a full 1-year guarantee.

In countries where the use of an 800 number is not practical, appropriate resellers will be used. Low product support requirements will aid in obtaining resellers, in part because Sun Microsystems has already tied up most of the VARs and resellers that are capable of supporting UNIX products.

Goals of the Seed Stage

The Seed Stage of the company is expected to require six to nine months. The goals for this stage are:

- Hire the core technical team (5 or 6 people), plus a controller/office manager.

- Develop the software architecture.

- Write the product requirements document of the NFS server product.

- Acquire a software development and LADDIS testing system.

- Develop enough of the software to demonstrate a prototype NFS server running on commodity Intel-based hardware.

- Determine the feasibility of using such commodity hardware for the first product. Determine if performance goals can be met.

- Obtain one or two senior marketing and sales team members.

- Obtain reliable feedback from potential customers to ensure that the first product is designed and positioned properly. Identify beta testers.

- Tentatively qualify hardware components and vendors.

- Identify hardware partner(s).

- Complete the business plan.

- Obtain Development Stage financing.

NFServer: Preliminary Specifications

A New Kind of File Server

The NFServer is designed from the ground up to be a dedicated NFS fileserver. Using an imbedded real-time system, instead of UNIX, it provides easy administration, high availability, excellent data integrity, and high performance.

Major Components

- Uninterruptible Power Supply (UPS)
- Fault-tolerant disk array (RAID) with 1 GB to 16 GB capacity
- Fsck-less filesystem for instant boot
- Single expandable filesystem partition; grows as disks are added
- Custom real-time kernel optimized for NFS
- Full-screen administration tool
- SNMP agent
- Optional second Ethernet interface
- Optional tape drive for backup

Major Benefits

- Easy Administration   SysAdmin complexity is minimized by eliminating UNIX, providing a single filesystem partition that expands as disks are added, and eliminating implementation-related configuration choices.

- High Availability   Single-purpose software (no UNIX, VM, or user programs), UPS, RAID, and instant reboot, provide an exceptionally high level of service availability.

- High Performance   Eliminating UNIX, and using optimized real time software that takes advantage of the UPS, provides the highest per-Ethernet throughput and lowest response times in the industry—as measured by SPEC SFS (LADDIS NFS performance benchmark).

- Data Integrity   UPS, RAID, and software design provide very low probability of data loss due to hardware of software malfunction.

- Trivial Installation   Simply plug in the NFServer (power and Ethernet), specify an IP address, and the NFServer is ready to use with its filesystem exported.

- Low Price   System cost is reduced by eliminating UNIX and the superfluous hardware it requires— leading-edge RISC processor, virtual memory, RAM, keyboard, and display. Entry price: under $10,000 list.

APPENDIX B
NetApp Company Values

Create a Model Company by:

Driving *customers'* success and earning their loyalty through products, services, knowledge sharing, and other solutions that further the appliance concept, delivering unparalleled value.

Providing our *shareholders* with exceptional value through predictable performance and significant growth in revenue and profits.

Attracting and retaining performance oriented *employees* who thrive in a challenging and supportive environment, and are recognized and rewarded for their achievements and contributions.

Developing and nourishing *partner*ships to deliver superior solutions for customers.

Maintaining good relationships with *neighbors* and communities where we work.

Trust and Integrity

Our interactions are based upon candor, honesty, and respect for individual contributions. We are committed to earning the trust and confidence of our teammates and to always acting for the absolute good of the whole.

Leadership

The role of leaders is to articulate and demonstrate our shared vision, values, and goals. Leaders transform individual effort into high-performance teams that are prepared for expanding roles and challenges.

Simplicity

We embrace the Einstein principle that everything should be as simple as possible and no simpler. We maintain simplicity in our internal processes and structures with objectives that are succinct, quantitative, and time bound.

Teamwork and Synergy

We achieve synergy through the skills and ideas of all participants. Through collaboration, we strive for win/win solutions to issues and problems. Personal success is realized through team achievements.

Go Beyond

We set extraordinary expectations and goals and believe in the joy of achieving significant results. We embrace creativity, risk taking, and continuous improvement, enabling us to make and meet aggressive commitments.

Get Things Done!

Glossary

AI (Artificial Insemination) A technique for getting cows pregnant without bulls.

AI (Artificial Intelligence) The science of getting computers to act "smart," to play chess, recognize language, drive cars, and so on.

all-hands meeting A meeting to which everyone is invited—everyone in a department, or even everyone in the company.

angel A wealthy individual who invests in start-ups. Angels often made their money from a successful start-up of their own.

Apache Software that lets a computer act as a Web server.

Auspex A competitor to NetApp that was founded in 1987 and went bankrupt in 2003.

backups Copies of data made in case something bad happens to the original. If you value your data, you should back it up at least once a week.

benchmark A performance test. There are benchmarks to test many aspects of computer performance.

beta testers Customers who try out a product before it is completely finished. When the beta testers are satisfied, then it is time to sell to real customers.

Board of Directors A group of people who oversee a company and its CEO.

business plan A document describing how a company plans to make money and grow. Start-ups write business plans to raise money from angels and VCs.

CEO (chief executive officer) The top boss in a company. Only the Board of Directors is above the CEO.

CFO (chief financial officer) The head of the finance department, responsible for budgets, spending, figuring out how much money the company is making, and so on.

chairman of the board The person in charge of the Board of Directors.

CIO (chief information officer) The head of the IT department, responsible for all information technology in a company.

COO (chief operating officer) One of the top two or three people in a company, reporting to the CEO. The roles played by COOs and presidents are highly variable, depending on the skills of the top people. See also *president*.

CTO (chief technology officer) The person responsible for guiding a company's technology strategy.

customer support department The group in a company that helps customers who have problems.

data center A big room or building designed especially to hold computing equipment. See also *enterprise data center*.

database A collection of organized data, like a list of customers, their credit card numbers, phone numbers, what they have bought, and so on. Also, the application used to create and manage this organized data.

direct sales A sales model where a company sells products directly to customers. When you buy corn at the farmers' market from the family that grew it, that's direct sales; when you buy corn at the grocery store, that's indirect sales.

EMC NetApp's main competitor, still several times our size. The initials came from the three founders' names.

engineering department The group in a company that designs and implements its products.

enterprise customer A very large customer, typically with thousands of employees and offices around the world. Enterprise customers have lots of money, but can be demanding and difficult to satisfy.

enterprise data center A large data center designed to meet the needs of enterprise customers. Serious ones have twenty-four-hour

staffs, security like a bank vault, and—in case of power failure—
enough diesel generators to power a medium-sized town.

Ethernet Most networks you can think of at work and at home are
Ethernet. If you plug a wire into your PC to get access to the Internet, that's probably Ethernet.

file server A system that lets users share files over a network, instead of storing them on a disk drive inside their computer.

Fortune 500 and Fortune 1000 Lists produced by *Fortune* magazine of the top 500 (or 1,000) companies in the United States,
ranked by revenue.

FUD (fear, uncertainty, and doubt) A sales tactic that large companies use against small companies: "Don't buy from them; they
might go bankrupt."

going public The process of converting from a private company
owned by a small handful of people to a public company whose
shares can be purchased by anyone. Also known as the IPO.

human resources (HR) department The group in a company
that focuses on people-related issues: recruiting, hiring, firing, payroll, benefits, and so on.

IPO (initial public offering) See *going public*.

indirect sales A sales model that involves a middleman, like a reseller. See *direct sales*.

institutional investor A company that invests large amounts of
money, like a pension fund or a mutual fund.

investment bank A bank that specializes in helping private companies go public, among other things.

IT (information technology) Computing hardware and software,
including laptops, PCs, large computers, the applications they run,
and the networks that connect them.

IT department (information technology department) The
group in a company responsible for information technology, running
payroll systems, billing systems, accounting systems, and so on.

Linux An operating system that competes with Windows and
UNIX.

magic See *pixie dust*.

mainframe A very large computer used in enterprise data centers. Companies are increasingly using smaller computers running UNIX, Windows, and Linux instead of mainframes.

marketing department The group in a company responsible for identifying customers, doing advertising and promotions to get noticed by them, developing partnerships, presentations, Web sites, and anything else that helps to sell the company's products more effectively.

mission critical Something that absolutely must keep working 100 percent of the time. The systems a company uses to deliver services to its customers are mission critical. The phone company's 911 service is mission critical.

monetize eyeballs To somehow make money by having a Web site that many people visit. In the dot-com boom, many Web start-ups measured their worth by how many people viewed their site (eyeballs); they figured this must be valuable, even though they had no idea how to make money from it.

MO (management orgasm) Steve Kleiman's term for the feeling that a manager gets after solving a really hard managerial problem.

network storage Storage that is out on a network, instead of on a disk drive in your computer. See *NAS* and *SAN*.

NAS (network-attached storage) A type of network storage that competes with SAN. NAS and SAN are a classic case of low-end versus high-end. Initially, SAN was faster and more reliable, but also much more expensive. Over time, NAS improved to the point where it is now a credible alternative to SAN for most applications.

network protocol The description of how two computers communicate over the network. For instance, the HTTP protocol lets one system see Web pages stored on another; NFS lets computers share files.

NFS (network file system) A network protocol that lets UNIX computers store data over the network; a type of NAS.

offsite A meeting held away from a company's offices, to avoid the interruptions and distractions that are inevitable when people are in their usual workplace.

operating system The software that controls a computer. Windows, Mac OS, UNIX, and Linux are all operating systems.

pixie dust The almost magical ability that some leaders have to solve problems and to inspire people to work with amazing productivity.

president One of the top two or three people in a company, reporting to the CEO. See also *COO.*

price-to-earnings ratio A measure of how expensive a company's stock is. Ten to thirty is common—maybe fifty or even a hundred for a high-growth company. Beyond that is crazy expensive.

professional services department The group in a company that provides for-fee services to the company's customers.

RAID Absolutely wonderful technology that our nontechnical customers don't really want to hear about.

recursion See *recursion.*

reseller A company that sells products made by other companies. A grocery store is a reseller. See *direct sales* and *indirect sales.*

response time How long it takes to do something. For a bakery, response time is how long it takes to bake one cake. If you know their response time, you still can't tell how many cakes they can bake in a day: they might have lots of ovens. See *throughput.*

router A piece of equipment that connects networks together. Cisco is the leading vendor of routers.

sales department The group in a company that sells its products.

SAN (storage area network) A type of network storage that competes with NAS. See *NAS.*

SEC (Securities and Exchange Commission) A federal law enforcement agency responsible for overseeing public companies.

Snapshots Absolutely wonderful technology that our nontechnical customers don't really want to hear about.

start-up A small young company that has not gone public.

sysadmin (system administrator) A person in the IT department who manages computers, networks, and applications.

terabyte Enough storage to hold about two million copies of this book; the total amount of storage in five or ten laptop computers. Technically speaking, it's one trillion (a million million) characters.

throughput How many of something you can do in an hour (or however long). See *response time*.

TO (technical orgasm) Steve Kleiman's term for the feeling that an engineer gets after solving a really hard technical problem.

UNIX An operating system that competes with Windows and Linux. UNIX often runs on big computers in data centers.

VC (venture capital) Investments made in small private companies. VC firms are similar to mutual funds, except that mutual funds invest in public companies.

WAFL Absolutely wonderful technology that our nontechnical customers don't really want to hear about.

Windows An operating system from Microsoft that competes with UNIX, Linux, and Mac OS.

workstation Like a desktop PC, except faster and more powerful. People sometimes use *workstation* to mean a desktop computer that runs UNIX instead of Windows.

Bibliography

Axelrod, Robert. *The Evolution of Cooperation*. New York: Basic Books, 1984.

Bok, Sissela. *Lying: Moral Choice in Public and Private Life*. New York: Vintage Books, 1999.

Christensen, Clayton. *The Innovator's Dilemma: When New Technologies Cause Great Firms to Fail*. Boston: Harvard Business School Press, 1997.

Diamond, Jared. *Guns, Germs, and Steel: The Fates of Human Societies*. New York: Norton, 1997.

Hamel, Gary. *The Future of Management*. Boston: Harvard Business School Press, 2007.

Heinlein, Robert A. *The Past Through Tomorrow: Future History Stories*. New York: Putnam, 1967.

Moore, Geoffrey. *Inside the Tornado: Marketing Strategies from Silicon Valley's Cutting Edge*. New York: HarperCollins, 1995.

Wright, Robert. *Nonzero: The Logic of Human Destiny*. New York: Pantheon Books, 2000.

Acknowledgments

Writing this book became an obsession, and I'd like to thank my family not only for putting up with me but for reading draft after draft after draft, each time providing additional useful feedback: Yen Hitz, Nancy Hitz, Jerre Hitz, and Ken Hitz. Thanks to Mira Hitz for her moral support even though she can't yet read (or talk). Special thanks to my mom for her good-natured acquiescence to the stories about her. Apologies to my mom for not including NetApp's green accomplishments and awards in the book.

My co-writer Pat Walsh taught me the difference between an author (creates with interviews and a tape recorder) and a writer (creates with a word processor and keyboard) and gave me many useful lessons on my still-unfinished journey from the former to the latter. Pat's obsession lasted even longer than my own, so Jeannine and Jack, his wife and son, had even more to put up with.

This book consists of the lessons and stories from many people who helped to create NetApp, so I'm particularly indebted to Mike Malcolm, James Lau, Charlie Perrell, Brian Pawlowski, Tom Mendoza, Dan Warmenhoven, Don Valentine, Helen Bradley, Steve Kleiman, Jeff Allen, and Rob Salmon, as well as Bruce Clarke, Bob Wall, Kathy Mendoza, Patrick Mulroney,

Varun Mehta, Brian Ehrmantraut, Florence Chan, Andy Watson, Mark Santora, Isabella Conti, Armen Varteressian, Kathy Bittner, and Laura Pickering. They all helped build NetApp, and in many cases also gave me direct feedback on the book. Bill Barnett, Chuck Holloway, John Morgridge, and their team of business school students at Stanford helped keep the history alive in my mind with lively classroom sessions and the case studies they wrote. Thanks to Lauren Dutton, Jamie Earle, Stephen Henkenmeier, and Jeffrey Eisen, who prepared and revised the case studies.

Thanks to the many people—colleagues, friends, and friends-of-friends—who read early drafts and gave me valuable feedback: Audrey Van Belleghem, Bill Barnett, Bob Pearse, Cathy Belleville, Christina Richmond, Dan Petersen, Dawn Yules, Don Bulens, Don "Pop" Petersen, Duncan Love, Eric Allman, Eric Brown, Ernie Baumann, Garth Goodson, Gene Jordan, Ian Barnett, Jamie Pesek, Jay Kidd, Jennifer W. Harris, Jodi Baumann, John McArthur, Judith Maurer, Kathy Hennessy, Kendrick Royer, Kevin McAuliffe, Lea Hirschfeld, Linda Pearse, Lola Moline, Marianne Wisner, Mike Rubin, Nina Love, Peter van der Linden, Randy Thelen, Rob Baker, Sanjay Vaswani, Scott Callon, Steve Herrod, Steve Watanabe, Suresh Vasudevan, Teri Allen, Tom Georgens, Tylie Petersen, and Warren Adelman.

And finally, there is a variety of support that goes beyond feedback without which a book cannot be completed. Thank you to my assistant, Kathy Bittner, my agent, Amy Rennert, and my editor, Rebecca Browning.

The Author

Dave **Hitz** likes to solve fun problems. He didn't set out to be a Silicon Valley icon, a business visionary, or even a billionaire. But he became all three. It turns out that business is a mosaic of interesting puzzles like managing risk, developing and reversing strategies, and looking into the future by deconstructing the past.

As a founder of NetApp, a data storage and management firm that began as an idea scribbled on a placemat and now takes in $4 billion a year, Dave has seen his company go through every major cycle in business—from the jack-of-all-trades mentality of a start-up, through the tumultuous period of the dot-com boom and bust, and finally to a mature enterprise company. NetApp is one of the fastest-growing computer companies ever, and for six years in a row it has been on *Fortune* magazine's list of Best Companies to Work For. Not bad for a high school dropout who began his business career selling his blood for money and typing the names of diseases onto index cards.

Dave Hitz co-founded NetApp in 1992 with James Lau and Michael Malcolm. He served as a programmer, marketing evangelist, technical architect, and vice president of engineering. Presently, he focuses on strategy and direction for the company. Before his career in Silicon Valley, Dave worked as a cowboy, where he got valuable management experience by herding, branding, and castrating cattle.

••

Pat Walsh (San Francisco) is the founding editor of MacAdam/ Cage, a publisher of literary fiction and narrative nonfiction. Known as an editor who specializes in discovering and developing new voices, Walsh has worked with dozens of first-time authors in fostering their written voice. Before MacAdam/Cage, Walsh was a reporter for the *San Francisco Chronicle* and authored *78 Reasons Why Your Book May Never Be Published* (Penguin, 2005).

Index